T0169534

Lights, Camera, Action

Advance Praise for
Lights, Camera, Action

"If you are in the public eye as an athlete, coach, media personality, blogger, realtor, or salesperson, you need to equip yourself with the tools to professionally express yourself on the highest level or least to a level where your speech matches your talent level."

—**Terry Nelson**, EXP Realty
Broadcaster Fox Sports Ohio

"A *must*-read for anyone who does public speaking, on-camera appearances, or live interviews. After a career working in federal law enforcement and the Intelligence communities, I became a national news security consultant. Amy's media coaching tips and skills prepared me to handle the fast-paced world of appearing on live, national TV. Her techniques gave me the confidence I needed to handle any on-camera situation. Training and preparation are the hallmarks of excellence in any field, this has never been as important as in today's fast-paced digital media world. Amy's techniques work!"

—**Michael Steele**, former US counterterrorism
official, national news security consultant for
NBC, CBS, CNN, MSNBC, and FOX

"I knew I needed to expand my media presence to the world stage, but for years, I resisted getting in front of the camera because it was uncomfortable. Then Amy Scruggs invited me to a bigger life as my on-camera coach and media strategist, and BOOM! I began to attract and land audiences with my ideal customers and partners, and replaced the butterflies with FUN! Today, whether you are a WFH mom or business baller, everyone needs a media coach in their back pocket - so get this powerball program of Amy's wisdom, experience and pizazz and hang on for the ride!"

—**Christian LeFer**, Founder/CEO, Instant Nonprofit

"Amy Scruggs has written a must-read for anyone seeking achievement in media communications, her coaching talent has made the difference in the success of our company. Read *Lights, Camera, Action* - and learn from the leader of the industry. Thank you, Amy!"

—**James Schafer**, Founder/Operations Director
Global Signmart

"As an entrepreneur, Founder of Talent Finders and being a publicist, PR specialist & running my own business, it's critical and significant for individuals to have media coaching to prepare them for the media and press, they need to have the coaching in order to maximize the results for PR. *Lights, Camera, Action* is a must read if you're getting ready to be on TV and in the media."

—**Kerrin Black**, Co – Founder of Talent Finders
Public Relations & Publicity Specialist

LIGHTS
CAMERA
ACTION

Media Coaching For Any Professional
in Today's Digital World

AMY SCRUGGS

NEW YORK

LONDON • NASHVILLE • MELBOURNE • VANCOUVER

LIGHTS, CAMERA, ACTION

Media Coaching For Any Professional in Today's Digital World

© 2022 Amy Scruggs

All rights reserved. No portion of this book may be reproduced, stored in a retrieval system, or transmitted in any form or by any means—electronic, mechanical, photocopy, recording, scanning, or other—except for brief quotations in critical reviews or articles, without the prior written permission of the publisher.

Published in New York, New York, by Morgan James Publishing. Morgan James is a trademark of Morgan James, LLC. www.MorganJamesPublishing.com

Morgan James BOGO™

A **FREE** ebook edition is available for you or a friend with the purchase of this print book.

CLEARLY SIGN YOUR NAME ABOVE

Instructions to claim your free ebook edition:
1. Visit MorganJamesBOGO.com
2. Sign your name CLEARLY in the space above
3. Complete the form and submit a photo of this entire page
4. You or your friend can download the ebook to your preferred device

ISBN 9781631954955 paperback
ISBN 9781631954962 ebook
Library of Congress Control Number:
2021930707

Cover and Interior Design by:
Chris Treccani
www.3dogcreative.net

Morgan James PUBLISHING

Builds

with...

Habitat for Humanity®
Peninsula and
Greater Williamsburg

Morgan James is a proud partner of Habitat for Humanity Peninsula and Greater Williamsburg. Partners in building since 2006.

Get involved today! Visit
MorganJamesPublishing.com/giving-back

To anyone that has overcome adversity and is using that experience to help others, I give you my gratitude.
I have so many great people that have come into my life over the years from all circumstances and careers that are survivors, difference-makers, and positive people who chose to not let challenges turn them negative. I love the everyday hero that chooses to do the right things, work hard, and empower others. This book is for you!

Contents

Acknowledgments

Thank you to my loving husband, Brad Galvan, for his instrumental role and dedication and for working with the publishing and editing teams in getting this project to the finish line.

Thanks to everyone on the Morgan James Publishing team for your trust and guidance as you helped walk me through this incredible journey, including the design team who created the greatest book cover I could have ever imagined.

To Tatiana Galvan, Cortney Donelson, and Alyssa Hanes, my wonderful editors, who spent countless hours transforming my manuscript into a polished story.

Special thanks to my children, who were willing to share me with this growing career throughout the years and supported the pursuit of my dreams. You have been my inspiration, and I hope to have modeled the drive to always keep moving toward your passions and purpose.

Foreword

A week prior to meeting Amy, a good friend and colleague asked me to consider hiring key talent around media if, in fact, I was committed to changing our approach to marketing. Going from a traditional print marketer to a video-based strategy was a big leap in 2016, but we knew it was critical to separate and differentiate our firm from other competitors. How would our small firm locate the right person to represent our *team* in a manner that would support our beliefs and culture?

Enter Amy Scruggs.

In our first meeting together, she shared her background in country music and how she had opened for some of the biggest-named talent in the industry, such as Clint Black and Trace Adkins. Additionally, she spoke about her desire to serve others and specifically expressed her appreciation and heart for the military. Based on her backstory, I felt she would be a great spokesperson for our organization and an unselfish *team* player.

With the benefit of hindsight, I can say that Amy has been all those things and more. She has developed into a shrewd businessperson with great instincts. Amy has definitely moved the needle for our business around our success in media and has served as both a media coach and spokesperson. Her creativity, coupled with her desire to help make others better, and her big-hearted approach to every project has made her an invaluable business partner. Her fingerprints are all over the success of our firm's marketing and media efforts.

In 2018, our company was sold to Mutual of Omaha Bank. One of the reasons the bank was impressed with our company was our unique approach to digital marketing through the use of video. Again, Amy had a big role in our overall digital media strategy and execution.

I have personally been most impressed by Amy's commitment to faith, family, and country. This commitment is apparent in all areas of her life. She has overcome much adversity in her remarkable life. Because of her ability to overcome obstacles in life, she can handle difficult situations with poise and grace.

The future of marketing is about storytelling via video delivery of a concise message. It can be intimidating, but like all things in life, it takes commitment, focus, and hard work to become proficient. With time, everyone becomes more comfortable and confident. The toughest part of any journey is often the first step. I believe Amy's book will bring you great insight around these important topics and deliver you great value for your time. Take that first step . . . and enjoy your journey.

Philippians 4:12–13

—Torrey Larsen, co-founder/EVP Mutual of Omaha Mortgage

Preface

Coming from my background of clawing to the top and marketing myself against all odds through several careers and a deep financial recession, I never would have dreamed that I would someday be writing a book about anything other than a memoir of my unconventional life. Yet here I am, bringing my heart and passion to you in these pages, sharing with you the proven tips, strategies, and techniques that I have learned after spending over twenty years as a business professional, recording artist, public speaker, TV host, and media coach. The skills I am about to impart upon you are guaranteed to help anyone overcome one of life's most prevalent fears: **being on camera and public speaking.**

I was the buck-toothed kid who did well in school but did not have a desire to be anything but a country music star. I practiced the national anthem on the fireplace hearth with a hairbrush as my microphone at an early age and bossed my grade-school friends (thanks Christie Moreland) into choreographing the *Footloose* soundtrack for backyard showcases. I even charged the neighborhood kids a nickel for the privilege of watching the performance.

Being a doctor, lawyer, or business professional didn't even cross my mind.

In high school, I was awkward and insecure and found my only stand-out talent to be my singing voice. I was in every choir, performance group, and drama they offered at Western Christian High School in Covina, California. I did try one year of girls' basketball; however, my five-foot-five-inch stature at that time and a lack of any coordination resulted in a disaster, the remnants of which are nothing more than a team jersey in a long forgotten memory box. Fast forward to a chosen path of having four kids by the age of thirty-two. I could not have ever imagined through the chaos of my life at that time the career that was about to unfold before me.

My first big break, and what I still consider a miracle, was reading the name on a Post-it Note given to me by yet another mysterious name on another Post-it Note that read: "Call this number, tell them I sent you, and don't look back." To this day, I could not tell you the name of the individual who handed me the note, but four weeks later, I was a wholesale account executive in Orange County, California, for CitiFinancial Mortgage.

My boss, Liz Montes, saw in me something I did not yet see in myself. She said, "I will train you and teach you everything I know." This one amazing woman saw past my inexperience and naivety, choosing instead to nurture my ambition and drive, ultimately launching my sales career. It was 2001, a time when the mortgage industry was booming, and conditions were ripe for me to learn all that

I could. Driven by gratitude for her confidence and investment in me, I worked even harder to make her proud. Within six months, I was the number one sales representative in the country for all of CitiFinancial.

In 2004, on a trip with my parents to Nashville, we met James Rea (a well-known A&R Rep on Music Row) on a whim that is still inexplicable to this day. Three days and a recording studio/producer visit later, my recording aspirations became a reality. I spent the next year flying back and forth to Nashville while still managing my thriving mortgage career. In 2006, as the next steps for my music career were beginning to unfold, I was diagnosed with a serious health issue that required major surgery. The recovery from this was slow and painful; simultaneously, the real estate and mortgage industry began to collapse. Wholesale mortgage was the first to go. My stable career and job were gone almost overnight.

James had taught me that they call it the "music business" for a reason. The only way to survive a crisis is to shift, set a plan, and keep moving forward. So a business plan was put in motion to pursue music full-time, putting forth the same passion, work ethic, and drive that Liz had taught me in my mortgage career.

Six months later, after driving around and personally delivering my marketing package to strategic music venues, I got a call from a casino in Camp Verde, Arizona, that said, "You have been chosen to open the Fourth of July concert for Clint Black." They told me the marketing manager told the deciding board members to "hire her;

she is tenacious." And so, my music career and touring path began.

Over the next few years, I crisscrossed the country, forging my way through countless gigs, musicians, and uncertainty, experiencing incredible highs, as well as overcoming equally difficult challenges (among those challenges was a drummer who insisted he be flown home in the middle of our tour, so I did, and we persisted nevertheless). I believe this was in the "surviving the music industry" handbook! Not to mention, this was with four kids in tow. This trying and rewarding season of my career saw me opening music concerts for some of the biggest names in country music and fulfilling my childhood dream.

During this time, I also fulfilled my dream of singing the national anthem at professional major league sports stadiums and events. Furthermore, these experiences opened the door for me to pursue my long-held passion for serving the military and veteran community. By 2009, I became the spokesperson for the American Veterans of California (AMVETS), speaking and performing at hundreds of military and veteran events on their behalf. It was life-changing work that molded me, not just as a performing artist but as a business professional, public speaking spokesperson, and community leader. My first radio-released song in 2009 was "Comin' Home," written by my friend and touring partner Dave Adams. It was a celebration song for our heroes coming home from the current war and for those who did not get a proper welcome home from wars before. By this point, my oldest son, Ryan, had stepped into lead guitar and was writing new music for us. At the time, I thought this was the greatest career peak I could have ever dreamed of. However, as every great infomercial always says: "But wait, there's more!"

In 2011, my contract with AMVETS ended. Hanging onto my home became impossible, and it was ultimately lost. Within weeks, our bass player and my dear friend, Fred, died suddenly of a heart attack. It was time to grieve, pull the plug on touring, shift, set a plan, and keep moving forward . . . again.

The real estate and mortgage industry was starting to revive at this point. It was the obvious choice for me to use my previous skill set that I had learned at CitiFinancial and start over again to rebuild financially. On a Thursday in August 2010, I was doing my last big show, opening for Trace Adkins in Santa Rosa, California. Four days later, on a Monday, I was in a cubicle starting my new position as an escrow sales representative in San Diego. I remember the fear and devastation as I made this transition back into the real estate industry, this time in a new city. Despite my uncertainty, I felt a peace inside that drove me as I felt I could build my life up again—that things would make sense again someday soon.

San Diego was magical and enlightening. I did not know anyone, and no one knew that I had just set aside my dream career as a touring artist. I simply put my head down and tried to figure out who the main players were in the San Diego real estate market, make friends, and, of course, ask for the business. After two years in escrow, I was excited to get recruited back into the mortgage side. I started my position as a business development manager for a sales team, and then worked for several mortgage lenders as I maneuvered through.

By 2013, I was back in the music saddle, headlining my first show with a full band for a veterans' organization fundraising concert and a Veterans Day concert back where I grew up in San Dimas, California. I also started to perform each year for the San Diego Association of Realtors for their gala events.

By 2017, I was standing on the home plate at Petco Park, singing the national anthem for the San Diego Padres, which I have done each year since for the Military Appreciation games. It is truly my home stadium now. I also had the career highlight and honor of performing at the ship commissioning ceremony for the USS Rafael Peralta on the Navy base in Coronado.

Pressing through the fears of starting over, taking on new challenges again, and always moving forward were the key ingredients to finding new success. Both of my careers had now come together as one. It finally made sense.

In January 2017, I received a call from a colleague. He said, "Scruggs, I need you to meet Torrey Larsen. I think you are supposed to work together." This was a life-changing call. I was welcomed to TV, hosting for *The American Dream TV*, *Operation American Dream*, *Lifestyles San Diego*, *Retiring Right*, and I became the media personality for what is now Mutual of Omaha Mortgage. This wild career journey packed with fulfilled and crushed dreams alike had brought me to my purpose. This true purpose, I now realize, is giving and caring for others, helping people overcome obstacles, and sharing hope when there seems to be none in sight. Media coaching was born from my desire to help my interview guests feel better and give more of themselves than they knew they had in them. It worked! Consequently, Media Coaching has created more joy, opportunity, and possibility than I could have ever imagined for myself.

Never giving up and a fundamental belief that the journey will always add the required "tools to the belt" have allowed me to grow and adapt to diverse situations and opportunities. I am thankful for each person who believed in me and brought me here and for each obstacle that kept me humble and moving forward.

I hope that you feel my passion, hear my sense of humor, and understand my dedication to your success in this book. If the awkward choir kid can do this, so can you!

Chapter 1
INTRODUCTION

Welcome to the "virtual you" journey.

As a kid in class, whenever I was called on to speak, I would freeze. I would think, "What the heck is wrong with me? Why am I so confident while singing but paralyzed when I have to talk in front of the class or adults?" My insecurities were numerous and crippling. I felt awkward and out of place. I longed to be more like the others who seemed so comfortable and confident.

When I began my first career in mortgage in Orange County, California, everyone was beautiful and drove a BMW as polished as their sales and delivery. I was certain I was going to get eaten alive. In reality, my team, bosses, and clients saw a woman who was competent and self-assured. They did not see that every time I walked into the office, I still felt like a twelve-year-old with braces. But Liz, who gave me the job and believed in me, gave me the confidence, patience, and training to succeed.

The success I experienced began to transform me; it started to change the way I viewed my strengths and created a platform for me to gain confidence. When speaking to professionals and presenting to top-earning mortgage brokers, I learned something unbelievably valuable: Suppress insecurity, project confidence, and with time and experience, that confidence becomes the new reality.

Another big confidence boosting transition for me was four years ago when I was given the opportunity to host *The American Dream TV* show. I once again found myself learning new skills on-camera. After spending the past twenty years in business development for the mortgage industry, then after the crash and becoming a touring recording artist, and currently working as a TV host for business leaders, I have had plenty of experiences conducting interviews on all media formats. As a TV host, I learned to be the interviewer—to ask probative questions—thereby helping others deliver their stories and, more importantly, their messages.

I have participated in hundreds of interviews with business professionals, CEOs, entrepreneurs, nonprofit founders, and community leaders. I witnessed first-hand how most people react when the camera comes on. The most common response is fear: fear of making mistakes, fear of how one looks, and fear of sounding inadequate on camera. These top-earning professionals relied on me as the host to make them comfortable and confident so that they could succeed in delivering their messages.

Before each interview, I help each person visualize what their message looks like, what it sounds like, and how we're going to wrap it all together into one coherent package. For those I have extended coaching time with, I provide advanced skills in body language, self-awareness, and messaging content. This success in helping others started my media coaching business, helping professionals become relaxed and confident, ready to master any media appearance.

This book is the compilation of all those "aha" moments from amazing people who benefitted from my skills, tips, and tricks to be their best. This book will have examples of other professionals, just like you, with their different concerns and anxieties, as well as success stories about being on camera.

This is what you can expect to do with me in the next chapters: I will be teaching you how to come alive on camera and deliver the message that you hear in your head. You know, that one that resonates when you are lying in bed wide awake. The one you hear so beautifully in your mind and that you know is perfect. Yes! That is the one. I will help you be so comfortable in your skin that you will be excited to share your message and story. You will not be thinking about what you look like or how you sound or if anyone will laugh at you or if you will fumble. You may fumble at first. Yes, it happens. It happens to me all the time. But guess what? I will help you learn how to not lose your focus and recover like a pro. I can help you maybe even find the humor in it and get a good laugh out of your audience. Sometimes, those moments end up resulting in your best interview yet.

In this journey of learning with me, I promise to help you be more ready, confident, and comfortable with embracing media and the virtual world. I will take you through the experiences, concerns, and discomforts of all the professionals I've worked with and their on-camera moments these past years. I will walk you through my twenty years of learning how to be confident—or at least look like I am when I am having an "off day." I promise to help you be concise and ready at any moment, regardless of what is going on in your life or around you at the moment.

I am going to help you find *you*. The *you* that you will grow to love and maybe finally *like* with a new set of eyes. I am going to teach you who you are from the lens of the camera . . . and we will blend the two of those so that both your view and the camera's view will not be different. I am going to give you real tools and tips to implement immediately, ones that will become new habits and communication skills. These will transform not only your on-camera life but also your communication.

I hate to see people miss wonderful opportunities due to the fear of being on camera. I received this email recently from a professional that quit the TV show I host. This person will remain anonymous. But this is what was said: "Dear team, being on camera is just not for me unless I have someone tell me exactly what to do and speak. I stumble all the time, and it keeps me up at night. So, this is just not the right medium for me."

For me, reading this was tragic! Missing golden opportunities for business, growth, new followings, and relationships because of fear that keeps a person up all night . . . it breaks my heart. I am on this mission to help keep this from happening to anyone else! Do not let this be you. Trust me to take you on this journey toward confidence in front of the camera.

On a trip to Hawaii, my husband, who is an avid diver, wanted me to do an introductory scuba course so I could join him on one of his dives. The problem was that I am deathly afraid of drowning. I am a horrible ocean swimmer. Put me in a pool, and I am fine. I grew up in pools; however, when I was twelve, I had a near-death drowning experience while swimming in the ocean off Newport Beach, California, and from that day forward, I have never conquered my fear of swimming in ocean water. My husband finally convinced me to sit through the course by assuring me that I would be safe and protected, that he and the instructor would be right by my side the entire time. Still unsure that I could actually go through with this, I agreed and sat through an introductory scuba course while signing my life away on a safety form! We then headed out on a boat into the clear, blue waters off the coast of Hawaii. That's when the anxiety hit me. It was like nothing I had ever felt before. I was sure that I was not going to be able to breathe with the air tank strapped to my back and that

I would have a panic attack underwater and drown. My mind had convinced me of this, and the entire ride out to the dive spot was like a death march for me.

As the boat anchored and everyone suited up, I felt worse and worse with each passing minute as it drew closer to my turn to jump into the water and leave the safety of our beautiful boat, basking in the warm sun and blue Hawaiian waters. I thought to myself, *what is wrong with just staying on the boat and watching everyone else go into the water? I can still have the same experience by hiding on the deck of the boat, right?*

Wrong. There was no way I was going to know how it felt under the water while standing on the deck of the boat. Was I going to drown? Most likely not. There were instructors, other divers, and my husband who were all assuring me that I would be safe and protected. I was still wrestling with just staying on the boat and accepting that this may be a life experience that was not meant for me.

Then something happened. There was a group of young women that were clearly all friends. They seemed small and petite, like young students. *How will they do this?* I thought. And then, suddenly, one by one, they jumped off the boat and disappeared under the sea in a flash. Their boat was empty. I realized at that moment that my ego did not want to allow me to be the only one left on the boat. My pride was too strong to go home failing—and not just failing but not even trying! I had to convince my ego to be bigger than my fear.

And I did it—I jumped off the boat! I went forty feet underwater and saw the tropical ocean floor of Hawaii. I DID IT! The terrified non-swimmer, who swore she would never swim in the ocean again—much less scuba dive—did it! Now, I have that memory and accomplishment to take with me the rest of my life. I was able to conquer my anxieties and fear and have used that moment as a launching pad to mentally prepare myself for success when I begin any new project outside my comfort zone.

Does this sound familiar? Have you felt this type of anxiety when asked to speak before a group of your peers or while making a presentation to your bosses . . . or maybe to a conference attended by hundreds of people? The anxiety is the same and so is the fear.

Lights, Camera, Action will show you how to gain the confidence, skills, and mindset for success in today's digital world. If you are ready to develop your practical skills and become a master of your own digital media, walk with me. Once we get to the other side, you will see a new, authentic view of yourself and how you can become a successful, confident part of this new virtual world! Jump off the boat with me! Let's do it! You will come alive on camera! Time to get started . . .

Here is my friend and client, Chad Coffman, sharing his experience on learning the skills and techniques that are ahead for you in this book. Chad is a great example of what can happen when you do the work. I asked him to share his experience with you.

▶ Well, where do I begin? Having been in the mortgage industry for more than fifteen years prior to meeting the great Amy Scruggs, I had done fairly well by my estimation. Knowing I had a thirst to hone my skills, I was—by a fluke—introduced to Amy. I was hosting an event, like we always would do, and she happened to be one of four guest speakers who presented that day. Amy happened to go last, and after hearing her story and listening to the passion this woman had, I was inspired. Amy had mentioned at some point that she had a joy in helping others grow, among many other things. I saw that we shared many of the same life principles. After our event had concluded, I was able to talk with Amy for just a bit. And if my memory serves me correctly—which most times it doesn't—it was for a week or so after that I lost contact with her.

After that week or so, I decided to reach out to her and just talk about the amazing experience I had listening to her story and let her know that I'd like to learn more about her and all that she does, which as you know, is a lot. That conversation turned into Amy Scruggs becoming my personal business coach. And not one of those "let's check in every week to see if you made your one hundred calls" coaches. They were intense two-hour sessions—sometimes two to three times a week (if my memory serves me correctly again).

I had a certain set of skills that I was proud of and that I had felt I had a pretty good handle on. However, there were a few I was in desperate need of help with.

After sitting down with Amy and targeting what my real needs were, we decided to address my desire to speak to larger crowds. This had always been a fear of mine. So much so that my anxiety would keep me from presenting things I was passionate about. Amy gave me the skills and the confidence I needed, and after two months of training, I was able to speak to a group of 500+ people. Let me tell you, the 500+ people were politicians, industry leaders, and some of the executives from my company. Needless to say, I was shaking in my boots. Not only did I do it, but I did it with vigor and a newfound confidence I would have never had unless I had Amy in my corner. She was so instrumental in my growth. Amy went from being a guest speaker in my office to my coach. I'm now blessed to call her my friend. If you ever have the chance to speak with this amazingly talented woman, do it, and savor every moment because it's not every day you will get an opportunity like this.

—**Chadwick T. Coffman**, Entrepreneur Regional
Director of Sales, CMG Financial

Thank you, Chad, for all your hard work! And now we get to help so many others through these upcoming chapters!

Chapter 2

DISCOVERY

Why do you need to become a media pro?

A lot has happened since the year 2000. I am sure that if you are reading this, and you are older than thirty-five, you will remember what it was like growing up around home videos. You may have even had that parent who would film everything you did, regardless of how seemingly insignificant it seemed at the time. There was a time when everyone would gather around to watch those treasured snippets of our lives, lovingly captured on film. It felt like magic. We'd laugh at our antiquated clothes, reminisce about family lore, and even remember those whom we had since lost.

The invention of the camera truly changed the way we remember the past and ultimately how we engage with the present.

Over the years, film and media have evolved, as have technology and societal standards. In the year 2000, we started to see dramatic changes and advancements in technology as it became cheaper and more widely available. We began to see smaller and smaller cameras and phones and more capable and portable audio and video equipment.

Over the past three decades, we have watched how video, television, and media have changed the way we live, interact with one another, and do business. When MTV came out, it changed music and media forever. By melding music and video together, our favorite artists came to life. I can only imagine the number of media training sessions they needed to go from being musicians who were recording in the studio or onstage playing music to then having to adapt to being on-camera rock stars. It changed the world for them and for us. Today, not just rock stars need media training—everyone does.

We started to see the changes in how videos could be used for business. Did you have a MySpace account? I did! I thought I was pretty tech-savvy for being able to modify my page using HTML codes. This was the start of social networking platforms. By 2004, Facebook had come along, and we had no idea what that would mean for us later. At first, we were all happy just to use it to find our high school friends and connect with our close contacts.

Stop and think for a moment about the evolution we have seen happen. Some of you may have been so focused on trying to keep up with technology that you've been missing the marketing opportunities that have been unfolding before your eyes. This is understandable, as trying to stay relevant and current with these fast-moving platforms is a full-time job in itself. Do you remember when you started to notice more advertisements beginning to appear on Facebook? Would you have thought then that this was where you were ultimately going to market your business? At this time, many of us were adapting to this new world slowly, trying to utilize telemarketing, mailers, and email campaigns.

Since the year 2000, we have seen how advancements in new technology continue changing how and what video is used for. You probably remember your first camera phone, watching with awe as those first grainy, pixelated photos sailed into your inbox. In an alarmingly short window of time, we went from using pagers to flip phones to text messaging. Eventually, the texts could send a picture, then a video, and then suddenly, we could use our devices to stream our lives in real time. Our world became interconnected, in real time, through digital media.

Fast forward to the present, and we now have a myriad of social media platforms on which to engage and create. TikTok, Snapchat, Instagram, Facebook, and twitter to name a few, and new apps are being created every day. YouTubers are making millions of dollars a year. Many of us have had to enlist the help of our teenagers to keep our heads afloat in this ever-changing landscape.

Then came 2020. The COVID-19 pandemic forever changed how we act, interact, meet, talk, and do business. Millions of people around the globe were forced to abandon their offices, cancel their business flights, and digitize conferences. Necessity truly is the mother of invention, and thus the virtual office was born. Zoom accounts, comfortable headphones, sleek microphones, standing desks, thoughtfully curated digital backgrounds, and (perhaps above all else) flexibility became the new tools of the trade.

At the time this book was published, the pandemic had begun to wind down, and the world began to return to work. However, the fundamental nature of the workplace will never return to "normal." The pandemic caused people to reconsider what is most important to them, to look long and hard at the sustainability of their work-life balance. For many, the new virtual office offers flexibility and often the opportunity to achieve more in a day that is no longer spent sitting in traffic or navigating airport security. Our new normal takes place on camera, whether we like it or not.

In addition to the advent of the digital workplace, marketing and advertising is now a world in which video is king and print is a rarity. Mailers, flyers, ads in local publications . . . all of these are still viable avenues for marketing oneself; however, their clock is ticking as the way we consume information becomes more heavily dominated by video. Web visitors spend 88 percent longer on websites that contain video, and video content gets 1200 percent more engagement than pictures and text combined. These kinds of statistics may be alarming, but they are not new. Video has been trending upward as the most valuable return on investment for the past several years. Video enhances the impact and shareability of email campaigns, Facebook and Instagram ads, websites, and testimonials. You can now even purchase digital business cards with personalized QR codes which send your audience directly to your social media accounts and website. Video is everywhere, and my hope is that after reading this book, you feel comfortable enough to take advantage of all of the many opportunities to put yourself in front of the camera.

Despite the prevalence of these technological advancements, and despite spending most of the last year behind a screen, many people still get bashful or turn their heads away from the camera. Even those who are eager to "Facetime" friends and family or upload a personal video to Instagram can be uncomfortable with being in front of the lens in any professional capacity. While the evolution of personal cameras and social media has trained us well to use videography as a tool for entertainment and personal communication, it has not trained us to use media as a tool to propel a thriving business. This is what I hope to do in the chapters that follow.

Hopefully by now, you are getting a handle on your social media and don't feel entirely lost in the virtual workspace. You may be doing a lot already. Perhaps you are rehearsing your recorded presentations and videos (even if you're also closing one eye in self-conscious hesitation as you reluctantly push "post"). You might have already downloaded a photo and video editing app to your phone so that you can refine your media and enhance your look. There may also be those of you who utilize social media scheduling apps, which allow you to schedule dates and times for automatic posting as part of your streamlined business plan.

Alternatively, you may still be in the beginning stages of mastering your social media presence. I work with plenty of thriving business owners and entrepreneurs who are skirting around the idea of showing themselves on camera, instead opting to create video content that does not include themselves. Some video is better than no video; however, the greatest return on investment comes from video content that depicts *you*: the confident, comfortable and charismatic executive you are.

I know that many of you may not yet feel confident, comfortable, or charismatic on camera. On the contrary, are you the person at a networking event who ducks out or hits the floor the moment when someone goes Facebook Live? Don't laugh—I have seen it many times! So many people are not ready for this live-streamed world that we live in. Do you feel like you are slowly getting left behind those who seem to love the camera or make it look natural? Believe it or not, most people do not like being filmed on camera. More people than not are afraid of how they look, feel, and speak on camera. So how are you ever supposed to market or get your message across if you are so focused on not wanting to be on camera?

Have you ever gone to a party or function that you really didn't want to be at, and others incorrectly perceived from your look that you didn't actually want to be there? Well, that seems to be what happens on camera for many professionals; no matter how polished you are in your face-to-face meetings and boardrooms, there is something that happens to many when the camera is on, which makes them appear as though they are on the camera begrudgingly, even if that isn't the case at all. If I'm describing you perfectly, don't feel bad. You are among the majority!

For most people, being on camera and public speaking are terrifying; discomfort is a lot more prevalent than you think. Even that popular kid in high school has most likely frozen in front of the camera. These new media demands have evened the playing field for us all—the cheerleaders, the athletes, the intellectuals, the choir kids . . . all of us will need to either learn these new skills or tread water in a world that expects us to swim. There is a common ground now that we all need to conquer, and I am here to help you do it. I love watching professionals come alive on camera and change how they see themselves and how they deliver their message.

It is easy to get stuck in our ways and settle in with technology that we have grown comfortable with. I cringe every time I need to do a phone upgrade because I know I have to learn a new system all over again. I am the first one to want to hang on to my old iPhone as long as possible to avoid the change. I liked my thumbprint and home button. What is this face recognition nonsense? Do I set it up with or without makeup, with or without glasses? As much as my kids like to make fun of me for being set in my ways on this, I have to accept that it is the same principle I am teaching you in this book. We must adapt to what is new and what can help us, even when it is uncomfortable. We will talk more in the chapters ahead about being uncomfortable, but for now, rest assured that I, too, have been known to resist change.

When I am public speaking, one of my favorite visuals to give is the navigation system in the car. Imagine me standing before you describing this situation: Picture driving along and you end up making a wrong turn, or there is a detour that takes you off the path, and now you find yourself lost. (Doesn't that describe our lives over and over?) Okay, back to the car. What is that excellent phrase the navigation computer voice repeats to us?

"Recalculating route."

How many times in our lives have we had to stop and recalculate our route? Life has a tendency to keep us on our toes and stray from the plan every now and then. Now, we may try to stay on a consistent path as often as possible, but detours, construction, dead ends, and flooded roads happen to us throughout the many seasons of our lives.

Those of us who can shift and adapt despite changes are those who have figured out how to recalculate the route and, more importantly, those who will make it to their destinations. Regarding rigidity with technology, and the understandable reluctance to adopt new ways, many of us have had to recalculate.

I have also had to make that shift, constantly.

On-camera skills are not just for music videos and movie stars anymore—or your teenager on TikTok or the sales professionals creating digital marketing content on the front lines of business. Being on camera has now become the new normal for almost everyone.

Athletes need media training, along with recording artists and authors. If a recording artist gets a record deal with a major label, it is required that they do media training prior to the album release; this has been the case for years.

My friend, Christian Okoye, the "Nigerian Nightmare," learned this skill in his years with the Kansas City Chiefs from 1987–1992. He came from Nigeria to play college football for Azusa Pacific University. He was thrown into a new country, a new sport, and a new life overnight. I would say that he made a pretty great career out of it, for sure! But getting adjusted and learning to be media-ready as an NFL professional was not easy and took some adjustment.

Another friend of mine is Terry Nelson. He is a college basketball celebrity, coach, analyst, media personality as broadcaster for Fox Sports Ohio, and a powerhouse real estate agent. He gave some great insight on why media training is so important:

▶ Why Every Athlete Needs Media Training

" . . . um . . ." (As they look toward the sky to gather their thoughts.)

. . . like I said before . . ." (This was my first question . . . when did you say this before?)

How many times have you heard an athlete being interviewed at halftime or the end of a game, and what comes out of their mouth totally changed the perception you had of that athlete? I often ask myself, *with access to resources the average citizen doesn't have, why don't more athletes get professional media training?*

One of my favorite things to do is watch post-game press conferences. To see a coach or an athlete grab the microphone, lean back, slouch down in their chair, and mumble words that are not clearly articulated is a forehead slapper.

Cars, jewelry, and houses will add to the eyeballs that are attracted to us as athletes or former athletes. Think of how much money parents are paying to have personal training for their athletic son or daughter. Twenty-five to eighty dollars per session, with multiple sessions per week. Parents know this will give their child an advantage to improve their skills so they can perform in big moments when the pressure is the greatest. There is a universal understanding in the sport of competition: repetition beats talent. Talented people tend to amaze people with the things they are able to do; it just seems natural to them. But hard work beats talent every day when talent doesn't work hard. Repetition is the great equalizer!

The great King Solomon once mentioned a timeless piece of wisdom thousands of years ago when he said it was better to be thought of as a fool than to open your mouth and remove all doubt. If you are in the public eye as an athlete, coach, media personality, blogger, realtor, or salesperson, you need to equip yourself with the tools to professionally express yourself on the highest level, or least to a level where your speech matches your talent level.

—Terry Nelson, EXP Realty, Broadcaster for Fox Sports Ohio

Erica English is the Director of Marketing for Mutual of Omaha Mortgage. She has an extensive background in corporate marketing and leading large executive teams. I asked her why digital marketing is such a key component to success for today's professional:

Traditional marketing has changed for the better, becoming more attractive through the social media and digital platforms, which can do so many new things for a business. Social media fosters brand recognition and creates business leads for your company, and that's just the beginning. It's also well known that digital marketing is very affordable when done right, compared to conventional marketing. An email or social media campaign delivers your message to a wider audience for a fraction of the cost. This helps marketers become more informed about their target audience's likes, dislikes, and interests so they can create a better marketing strategy to attract customers in real time. Especially when it comes to video content, audience attention must be captured within fifteen seconds to create engagement, or you'll run the risk of losing consumer interest altogether.

Whether it's a voice-over, video, or digital ad, it's of utmost importance to tell a story from start to finish, capture the highs, and end with a strong call to action. With these things in mind, it's clear that digital marketing is the way to capture your audience.

—**Erica English**, Director of Marketing,
Mutual of Omaha Mortgage

Jeff Blackwell has a long track of success in mortgage lending, leading and training large corporate teams. I asked him why it is important for professionals to shift into mastering media marketing skills in today's climate:

Video conferencing and messaging have never been more valuable. The business world demands it, and it has changed the way we do business forever. The confidence to do such things is something not everyone is born with (very few, in fact), but it is something we must learn. In 2019, I may have "hosted" three virtual meetings; a few months into 2020, I now "host" three to five per day. I do everything from "coffee" meetings with recruits to full-on training sessions that last several hours over the course of several days. Without the knowledge and training to do these, I would be out of business.

—**Jeff Blackwell**, VP of Production, Synergy One Lending

Whatever business you are in, I am here in these chapters to be your personal media coach. I want to help you be confident and deliver your message! I want to help you be *you*!

Chapter 3

SELF-AWARENESS

Have you looked at yourself lately?

Self-awareness can be a big, broad statement. There are so many ways that we try to be self-aware, or are at least willing to be. Hopefully, we are aware of how we treat people, how we speak with our loved ones, what kind of spouse, parent, and colleague we are, what kind of friend we are, and how we take care of our health.

But self-awareness in body image and how we speak and communicate a message is the next level of self-awareness to reflect upon. In the following chapters, I am going to help you be aware of things you may not have thought of before. I am going to help you discover some aspects of yourself that you will eventually come to know inside and out. Let's start on this self-awareness journey as we tie it into your life on camera. I promise you will see how this comes together and how you are going to become confident in a way that may even surprise you. In my experience, self-awareness and confidence are the two largest deficiencies among my clients, the two largest blockages to being comfortable on camera (including on Zoom and Skype). Have you ever played back a video of yourself and thought, "Is this what I look like? Is this what I sound like?" Have you noticed that these preoccupations can cause you to lose focus on what you're trying to say? These insecurities can also detract from your ability to focus on what others are saying.

Alternatively, there is such a thing as being "too" comfortable on camera. For fun, go to Google or YouTube and look up, "Zoom fails." It is eye-opening to see how many funny outtakes and inconceivable things people do on their home computer while participating in online meetings. When that camera is on, *you* are on. People are watching.

I was recently in a group meeting, and I won't name names, but one participant kept getting up to get food and then would stand in front of the computer with only his belly staring right at the camera. We do not need to see that! That is unprofessional and distracting. And I can't count the times the camera is angled right up at people's noses or the ceiling. Or my favorite—being able to see only half of a person's head because they are not framed correctly. Another Zoom clip shows a woman in a work meeting who forgot her camera was on as she set it down on the bathroom floor facing toward her . . . you can picture what happened next. Another person got up from his desk, thought his camera was off, and turned around to scratch his backside, repeatedly, in front of the camera, in full view of the other participants! People! *Oh my gosh.* These things would never have taken place in the office! So at your desk with the camera on, you need to be as polished and presentable as you would be in person. Self-awareness has many layers. These examples of Zoom failures are only one.

So here is the question: Do you know who you are? When you see a video or a photo, are you the one that says, "Is that what I look like?" and "Is that what I sound like?" The stark reality is, yes, you do!

I want you to think for a moment about your loved ones. Choose one—a friend, family member, or anyone who is top of mind for you. When you look at their face and body language, without words, can you tell when they are tense or sad? Can you tell when they are mad before they even say it? Focus for a while here with me on how they look. Picture their bodies tensing up when they are scared or angry. How does that look? What are those tell-tale signs that reveal their inner feelings to you? What about when they are confused about what you are saying? How does their brow look, and their mouth? What are their eyes saying? Think about every aspect of this person's body language as you deeply digest all the mannerisms that you are able to notice and read. For you parents out there, think of when you see your child excitedly running down the school path to get to you at the end of the day. Can you see when they have something exciting to share? Can you sense when they are sad before they even say so?

We naturally become so enmeshed with our close loved ones that we feel we are experts on them sometimes. I am sure we are all guilty of being mind-readers sometimes, convinced that someone feels a certain way based solely upon our interpretation of their body language. Now, they may not be aware of the messages they are inadvertently sending, but as the recipient, aren't you?

What would happen if you were able to know your own body language as deeply as you know that of the loved one you were just picturing? I will get you to know what message you are sending in every communication, verbal and nonverbal. You will know yourself *that* well. It's possible! You will find out who you are and become so aware that your on-camera and your off-camera personality become the same person.

While hosting hundreds of business professionals on *The American Dream TV,* the most glaring observation I made is that most of them did not know how to present their face. They weren't sure how to smile or which facial expression to hold, and they would attempt to perfect their posture until their bodies finally resigned, confused during the final minutes before going live. This can result in a disastrous recipe for losing your focus, your message, and yourself at that moment. This can be solved. You can learn how to override this and have everyone else saying, "Wow, you made that look so easy."

One of my clients who has grown the most in this area is Angela Caliger from Newport Beach, California. She is an amazing real estate professional who has a successful background in business. Being in Newport Beach, alone, compels anyone to exude confidence to keep up in the highly competitive climate. As we started working together, I noticed she had confidence when speaking, and she could clearly articulate her message for the upcoming TV segments she was preparing. However, the work we needed to do was in with her recognition of her own body language and facial expressions. She knew what she wanted to say, but when the camera came on, her energy dropped, and her expressions weren't as animated as her regular speaking was off-camera. Self-recognition and memorization allowed her to start delivering in a much more natural and energetic manner on her TV segments. I watched her on-camera delivery grow exponentially through her recognition of her facial expressions and body language. She became familiar with her own facial expressions, made the shift to presenting those that make her look as calm and confident as she feels, and never went backwards in her skills after our work. I get so excited when I see her marketing videos and online presence as she has clearly mastered her craft now! I love seeing the work come alive. Angela definitely came alive on camera.

Let us discuss body language now. One guest on my show was ready and sitting at his seat. He was properly lit, microphoned, and ready to start filming. The problem was that his body was so stiff that his face showed how uncomfortable he was. This discomfort rippled throughout the rest of his body, and it was impossible to miss. I wanted so much to help him relax.

Now, the opposite is too relaxed. No one likes to see someone reclining too casually in a formal setting or a laptop webcam facing the belly as someone lays down to participate in a meeting. This is the polar opposite of those whose discomfort is nearly palpable through the screen. So how do you find the right balance, demonstrating that while you are calm, poised and confident, you are also professional and polished? Well, think about how you stand when you walk into a meeting, a party, or an event that you are excited to be in. We all stand up straight when someone important walks up to us, don't we? That power stance that we learned to have in childhood, when everyone's posture suddenly corrected the moment the principal walked in unexpectedly.

Think about how you stood when you were young, and the teacher called upon you to stand up and answer a question. Did you slump over the desk, stand stiff, or become stone-faced? Hopefully, you did not do any of those. Think about how you stand or walk into the house when you have great news you are sharing. Your body will naturally take a position of enthusiasm. Your shoulders, neck, arms, and hands will all reflect the joy you are feeling.

Stop for a moment and imagine what it feels and looks like to be happy, calm, and sure of yourself. Think of a time in a photo or video that you saw yourself like that. Picture yourself being able to turn that on at any time you want to. Many people are not aware of how they stand even in a grocery store line. Start using your "confidence at a party" stance when you are at the store or talking to the neighbors at the mailbox. See how that feels different. Take notice of how your shoulders feel and what your back and legs are doing. Then repeat, repeat, repeat!

This can become your primary way of standing—or at least when you're not doing it you will start to become aware of it. Pay attention to what your body is doing when sitting at the table for dinner. It is most likely how you are sitting on your Zoom calls. Make new habits around the house, at your desk, and even in the recliner. Make sure you practice good posture and are not slumped over. Be attentive when you straighten your shoulders or hold in your torso. We all love to relax and unwind, but this should not be how we present ourselves to everyone else. In today's virtual world, this is the first thing that people see on the screen. If you can become this familiar with your positions, posture, and body tension or relaxation, then you won't have to think about it when the camera is on.

Next is your face. *Expressions* show everything. If I am telling you the most exciting story, yet my face seems unenthused or I show fear in my eyes, then I am not delivering my message correctly. I am going to talk about your resting face in the next chapter, so keep your face top of mind.

Let me give you an example. During a studio Skype interview, I had a top-earning professional gentleman who was articulate and joyful and smiling the entire time we chatted before filming started. As soon as the camera went on, I made his introduction and turned the first question to him. During those ten seconds, he had turned to stone, and he stayed that way the entire interview. His face was frozen for five minutes! No expression or emotion, and sadly, his message was lost. We have all heard the term "deer in the headlights." In my experience, after hosting hundreds of on-camera interviews, that seems to be the most common problem that happens to people, and our poor friend here is an example of the tragic consequences. Exercises for self-awareness can make a difference in your preparation for media. Here are a few easy ones to start with.

Ask for Honest Feedback

Ask friends and family to start telling you what your facial expressions are saying when you are together. Ask them to tell you what they think your body language and face are saying to them. What message are you giving without words? You might be surprised to find out what they say.

Mirror Exercises

Spend a few days or a week and start making the majority of your phone calls in front of a mirror. This includes phone calls to family, friends, clients, and everyone. It will help you see what your natural responses to different conversations and emotions are. These will be the same faces and reactions that will happen on camera. This is the first exercise I have all of my clients do as when they work with me. Dancers practice in front of the mirror to perfect their performance and memorize every movement.

It is just as powerful of a tool when learning how to see yourself and master your own expressions. Even when you are in a parked car, pull down the mirror, and be on the phone in front of it. Pay close attention to your natural communication face. The more you know, the easier it is to control and recognize this part of yourself.

Play Back Your Footage!

Repetition is your best friend here. Play back your personal and professional videos as often as possible. Try to look at them through the eyes of a stranger. Critique the same way a stranger might or as though you would critique a colleague. Give yourself an honest review. Be sure to include in your review areas in which you excelled (give yourself credit where credit is due!) as well as areas in which there is room for improvement.

Sports legend John Robinson has had an incredibly long career as a championship head coach for the University of Southern California and the LA Rams. Over his career, he has worked with hundreds of college and professional athletes. And now in his eighties, he is the current head coach advisor for the 2019 college football champion team, Louisiana State University. I asked John about the importance of watching the after-game footage. Here is what he shared:

"Watching the game footage is the number one most important coaching and training tool used, period. The number one."

John went on to share how working with the teams by viewing the game footage impacted every aspect of coaching and training for success. He said it is crucial to learning the skills of the game. They analyze every aspect of the tape to make strategic decisions and game-planning is based on their assessments. They learn the fundamentals of the game through the tape and do deep analysis of each game. They use slow-motion viewing to hyper-focus on specific plays to improve, change, and expand to find the winning coaching tools.

Watching the tape wins games. I am so thankful to Coach John for his insight and input on this critical part of coaching teams to championships. Imagine how your media and speaking "game" can go on to the championship level with this kind of discipline. We all dislike seeing ourselves played back, but this new habit and created awareness will be the most beneficial exercise for change.

Chapter 4

FIRST IMPRESSIONS

Don't trip into the room with the wrong face on.

M ost people talk about and are familiar with the importance of "first impressions." Some more than others know the power of it, and some write entire books about the power of the first impression. My mentor and the amazing best-selling author of *How to Make People Like You in 90 Seconds or Less*, Nicholas Boothman, wrote his book on how to do just that: how to get someone to like you in ninety seconds. If this were not a hot topic and lifelong skill, then his book would not still be on the best-seller list twenty years after he wrote it. It has endured because the message is powerful and relevant. I highly recommend you read the entire book to master this part of your growth and training, as first impressions are that important. I am going to give you some things to think about right now, though, to bring this awareness to mind.

We leave a first impression nearly everywhere we go: with the checker at the grocery store, opening a door for someone with their hands full, a smile and nod at the jogger treading past us—there are endless opportunities to leave a first impression. In this new virtual world, so many of these first impressions take place on a screen. This means we need to be even more self-aware and more prepared than ever before. There is a camera on nearly every device and, thus, the ability to record more first impressions than ever before. I am going to show you how to master yours. I am continually growing and evolving in this area too. My advice to you is to stay open to this type of growth as well.

We are all guilty of forming lasting opinions around first impressions. When you are sitting in a coffee shop, at the dog park, or waiting for a friend at a restaurant, do you people watch? I do, and I find it fascinating. I naturally wonder about the people around me. What are they thinking about, where are they going, are they in the middle of a tragedy, or are they having the best day of their lives? When someone walks by me, I form my own idea as to what state of mind they are in. Do you notice someone in public that just looks obviously angry, sad, or happy? This is called "your resting face." Ah, the resting face! It is a term that can change the way you see yourself and others.

Notice the resting face. It is truly the first impression! It leads the body! It tells the rest of me how to respond. Our faces can tell a thousand stories and many times, your face is telling a story that you did not intend to convey. It is saying something without even knowing it.

My friend's husband has always had a very grumpy resting face. She tells me all the time that he just seems in a state of perpetual annoyance. So she feels disconnected from him and does not always want to approach him about her day or her thoughts. Finally, she asked him why he was always so annoyed. Not surprisingly, he said that he wasn't annoyed at all. He was happy! It's hard to believe, though, that his resting grumpy face is actually a happy face. He had no idea that he was giving off a completely different message to those around him. At social gatherings, when others wouldn't readily approach him, he would think it was simply because people were already chatting in their established cliques or simply didn't want to talk to him, despite being very likable. He just did not know that his face was sending a different message—a distinct first impression that he never imagined.

You are reading this book, and therefore, I now consider you one of my friends and clients! I never want this to happen to you. I want you to know that you can give the right message the first time, every time. And in the upcoming chapters, I am going to show you how to do it even on your "off days" when you don't feel like yourself. I am going to show you how to have great first impressions in everyday life, regardless of your circumstances. I am going to get you there!

Now, I would like you to meet my friend Juliann. Throughout my career, I have met and worked with amazing people from all walks of life. And it is especially great when one of these amazing people I meet becomes a true friend. I had the honor of working with Juliann Ford through a nonprofit foundation, Future Legends, which provides scholarships and mentoring to college students. Juliann is an expert in etiquette training, manners, social skills, and the power of the first impression. I don't want to give away too much, but when you hear her story, it could be life-changing. What is fun for me is that I had the privilege of doing some media projects with her. She is just like the rest of us, still getting used to speaking on camera and becoming comfortable with this new virtual media world. Juliann is the essence of grace, style, and class. I will let her share her experience of being thrown into a powerful "first impression world" as the daughter-in-law of President Ford.

Researchers have found that a first impression is made within the first seven seconds of meeting someone new. When you meet someone for the first time, they are taking a rapid inventory of how you walk, your smile, your handshake, and how you present yourself. They are deciding if they can trust you, if you are genuinely nice, if you want to know you—so many questions are answered in those first few critical seconds based on what they see, and more importantly, how you make them feel.

> *"Please will forget what you said. People will forget what you did. People will never forget how you made them feel."*
> **—Maya Angelou**

In today's world, a first impression can be made via social media. Being aware of how you present yourself on Facebook, LinkedIn, Instagram, or Twitter can expose you to more people than you will ever meet face-to-face.

Your handshake used to be a big part of your first impression. Nowadays, people can Google your name and check your interests, work history, friendships, and photos!

A few years ago, I was invited to an event by someone I had never met. During our introductions, the host let me know she had "Googled" me. At first, I was a bit taken aback but then realized she just wanted to get to know me better and have "talking points" when we saw each other in person.

I highly recommend that you check your social media on a regular basis to make certain the image you want characterized is the one that is actually represented online. In today's world, your first interview may be conducted via video call so your online presentation is imperative if you want to express yourself as authentically as possible.

Networking events are typically full of "first impression" opportunities. Second to dressing appropriately for the event, I recommend my clients confidently walk into the room as if they were the host. Walking in and shuffling over to the corner without making eye contact with anyone is not a good way of meeting potential professional and social contacts.

Being overconfident is also not the best way to make a first impression. We have all been to an event where someone barges into the conversation and takes over with their bold and sometimes boisterous behavior. Balance and awareness are key when networking. Making those around you feel comfortable will mean more to them—at least at first—than what you are trying to promote.

I was invited to a high-level private reception prior to the more public larger event. Dressed appropriately and having a "good hair day," I smiled confidently as I began the security clearance portion of the evening. There was a feeling of anticipation as we waited our turns to be screened and wondered, *Who else has been invited?* Would we know anyone else attending? Imagine walking into a room where everyone is a VIP, each person's resume more impressive than the previous. That was this event. Both men and women were handsomely attired; the room was alive as they engaged in conversation and the last hour of sunlight peeked through the west-facing windows.

Like me in this situation, perhaps you've attended an event where all of a sudden, you realize that you are the least important person in the room. Listen to *the other* little voice in your head, the one reminding you that you were invited for a reason, so stay confident and make your introductions. After making a few new friends, you'll become comfortable and relax without any concern about how important the other guests are.

Typically, one final couple arrives (late, but not fashionably so), and the room atmosphere suddenly changes. You wait your turn to make your introduction, and then *it* happens. Your hand reaches out to shake (firm grip, two pumps); you smile and make eye contact—everything you have done all evening. That's when it happens: they offer their hand but look past you to see who else is in the room. Your confidence starts to slip and you step away. You notice that others who had previously been laughing and enjoying conversation start speaking softer and are not as animated. The tone of the event has changed. We've all experienced this rejection or something similar—just try not to be that person who makes others feel uncomfortable.

An athletic student of mine had been traveling cross-country every weekend one summer. A highly-recruited young man, he had been invited to attend elite showcases. His schedule was filled except for one weekend. It would be his one weekend to spend at home without any commitments. Then the call came: could he be available . . .? Since he lived on the other side of the country, he did not consider the request. But they called again and explained the organization would fly him from wherever he was; they would be paying for his accommodations and would be outfitting him with all the equipment required. After assuring him that he would be compliant with any athletic rules, he accepted their invitation to be one of fifty young men in the country hand-picked for this exclusive experience. He was advised to keep this invitation secret until the weekend of the event, where he was then encouraged to post everything on social media. It was a weekend, he says, that he would never forget. After the event, he remembered his lesson of always thanking those who helped and/or made a memorable impression. He wrote thank you notes to three individuals who assisted in making his experience extra special. The following year, my student received a second invitation, even though he had been previously told this was a one-time-only offer. He will never know if it was his athleticism that prompted that second invitation or the gratitude he shared through his thank you notes.

Following these guidelines will help you make your best first impression:

1. **Be confident.** Don't be afraid to say hello to new people.

2. **Smile.** Especially when first meeting someone.

3. **Make eye contact.** Stay focused on the person you are speaking with and not on anything (or anyone) else to avoid making them feeling unappreciated.

4. **Maintain proper posture.** Body language can tell someone a lot about your mood and confidence level. No slouching—it gives the impression of in-security and defeat.

5. **Don't fidget.** Keep your hands to your side or in your lap.

6. **Relax and be yourself.** Posture is very important; sit up straight but not stiff—you don't want to look like a robot.

7. **Dress appropriately.** Think about what you wear and the cleanliness of your clothes.

8. **Remember the names of the people you meet.** When introduced, use the person's name and con-tinue using their name throughout your conversa-tion. People feel valued when you remember their name.

9. **Concentrate on getting the person to talk about themselves.** This will show that you are interested in them.

10. **Never brag.** This includes name-dropping.

> —**Juliann Ford**, founder of Manners Prep,
> daughter-in-law of President Gerald Ford

Thank you, Juliann, for your wonderful insight.

We all create a first impression when we meet others. I would start fine tuning your first impression by asking your closest friends this question: "What was your first impression of me?" Wouldn't you love to actually know? Those who are close to you should not mind giving an honest answer. Their answers may surprise you. They may tell you that their first impression of you was drastically different than how they know you to be now. You may discover that your first impression communicated something that you did not intend.

Go back and look at some pictures and videos from the past and focus specifically on how you appear. Are your videos different in the friend, family, and home life categories than they are in your work life or networking life? A powerful exercise is to go back and watch the footage, old and new. What did you like, what did you not like, and what would you change?

I am not implying that you should change your personality or who you are. I want to make sure I am clear about my recommendations. It is a true discovery of yourself: the *you* who is *already* there. The first impression is showing the best *you* every time, the first time.

Practicing is the key. By this point, you are becoming aware of your body language and your facial expressions. You are more aware of what you notice in others. Now it's time to step up your game and make note of the impression you leave on others. This means practicing with each new encounter, every Zoom call, and every trip to the store. Be aware of how you greet people. If you're shy, that's okay! But maybe soften your face and have a genuine, natural smile! If you have a big voice and bigger personality, perhaps just be aware of those you are greeting and reign it in a notch (this is one I am constantly practicing). I am a big personality, and I need to be aware of it so I don't launch it all at someone in the first ten seconds of our meeting one another.

Begin with a deep breath. As you're about to greet someone in person or online, breathe all the way in first and then feel how your face responds. Notice how it will soften your face and your brow. Keep your eyes smiling. Are you strong and confident? Whatever your initial message for the first impression is, make sure it is the right one for the encounter!

If I am being pulled over for a traffic ticket, I probably want to have soft body language and be smiling with some humility. If I am walking in a parking structure alone at night, I better have my power-stance on—especially as a woman—and have my eyes focused and a confident stride with purpose. I do not want to look like a potential victim. I want my first impression to anyone who may wish to harm me to believe I won't be an easy target.

Another way to gauge how you are doing is to notice if you're getting a different response from people at the first meeting than you normally do. Reflect for a bit on what you perceive people's current response to you is, and later, I think you will see a change. Being aware of, and even documenting those changes, can really help. If you have on-camera webinars, notice the others and how they respond to your introduction or initial opening lines. If you are in-person, observe if others are endearing a little more to you or curious as to who you are and what you care about. I will help you with that message in the upcoming chapters. But for right now, notice your body and face and the messages they are sending during each encounter. Go to the store today, greet the checker, and see how he or she responds. Was it your usual self? Challenge yourself to be aware of your posture, face, and body. One step at a time, your self-awareness will create new first impression moments.

Chapter 5

IMPORTANCE OF THE MESSAGE

Messaging to a world with the attention span of a goldfish.

Monika Deroussel is an amazing woman who came to the United States from Slovakia and was on the Slovakian national running team, training for the Olympics. She received her degree from a university known as the "Harvard of Slovakia."

She arrived to the US in her early twenties only to find out that it did not recognize her degree. So she started over again, going on to earn a second four-year degree. She continued to run competitively while immersing herself in our English-speaking culture in Chicago. Upon graduating, she was hired by 3M and started at a six-figure salary.

Within a few years, she was happily married, adding children to her family, and had a successful, blossoming career with 3M. In one of life's unexpected turns of fate, her husband was suddenly transferred to a job in Cincinnati, Ohio.

Monika had to leave her career behind to move to a new town with her husband and children and start over yet again. She decided to begin a new career in real estate and, as she tells it, the first few years were rough. But as with anything, utilizing determination, consistency, and discipline, we can achieve what we put our minds to. She did just that and grew her business until she was the top-selling agent in her city. It came as no surprise when this amazing powerhouse joined *The American Dream TV* to escalate her visibility and propel the growth of her business using digital media. However, she quickly realized: "I don't have media training for this! I sell homes . . . what do I know about being on camera?"

So we worked together on the tools and techniques that I am sharing with you here. The outcome was that Monika not only mastered the art of being comfortable on camera, but she gained confidence, became an expert in articulation, and delivered her message effectively and professionally! How did she do this? Practice! She has overcome the uncertainty of public speaking and now delivers a message in four minutes or less, week after week. Her business is thriving! She is amassing a growing, productive team and is still the number one agent in her region. Honing her passion for real estate and coupling it with her naturally gregarious nature, she was able to overcome her fear of being in front of a camera and the true Monika came out! It has been incredibly rewarding for me to know that I have had a hand in helping her business thrive. She is an excellent testimony to the power of practice and perseverance in mastering your message and becoming a part of the media world. So much so that she took her media presence to another level and launched her own podcast. Mother of five, professional, national athlete, team leader, and now digital media master! She is among my favorite media success stories!

You are also capable of this kind of transformation! Now, let's jump into your message. The art of the message is powerful. Whether it is fun storytelling, educational, or emotional, your story can move people to know who you are and what you have to say.

Have you ever been stuck at a party with an overzealous person who has you cornered and doesn't know when to stop talking? They don't realize that any message they are trying to give you is now lost because you've tuned out and are simply searching for an exit.

Have you tried making conversation with someone who won't answer with more than one sentence? It can feel like pulling teeth. They are definitely not delivering their message, either.

Where do you think you stand between those opposite ends of the spectrum? The goal is to have your clear and concise message prepared for any communication situation you in which you find yourself. We don't want your audience to tune out before you get to the point you're making. It happens! We are all guilty of missing our mark at some point during our adult lives. But we can minimize the changes . . .

Let's take a look at some sample categories. Make sure you have a clear message. Are you trying to market to a potential client? What are the main points you want to come across to them? Having those bullet points in your head will help keep you from dancing around the point and possibly droning on, losing your audience. I like to pick on our close relationships because it is such a beautiful practice ground for mastering this. Getting your messaging through in your personal life will spill right into your on-camera life.

One great way to learn how to message is through storytelling. It is a powerful way to deliver what you are trying to say.

Example topic: I went to the beach, and the stairs are steep.

Storytelling for that topic could look like this:

After a beautiful day on the beach, relaxing and letting all the world wash off me, it was time to pack up and make my way up to the car at the top of the cliff. On the way down, I felt so energized as I hauled my chair and blanket and belongings down to the white sand where a day of peace, sun, and relaxation awaited me. Now, I feel the sting of the sun on my skin, the chair on my back feels like a razor blade, and my belongings seem twenty pounds heavier than they did on the trip down. The sleepy state of my eyes and body are a normal response to the ocean air and gentle breezes. I return to the staircase to exit, and I notice how high the cliff is. One step at a time, it feels like the stairs are growing in number under my feet. I stop halfway to catch my breath. I do not remember the stairs being this steep on the way in! After what feels like thirty minutes, I make it to the top, and it feels as if I have summited Mount Everest! Wow, those stairs were steep.

Your message may just be about something simple, but putting some color into it can have your viewer or listener living it with you! It is finding a way to make them a part of what you are sharing. We tend to talk "at" people when we are sharing—or especially selling.

Starting with a question is powerful. The listener can then think about whether or not they identify with what you are asking. They are already going into their brain database to find a common touchpoint or experience to live this with you. Then, they are in your same message space. They may find a common thread they want to retain, reshare, or experience with you. This is a powerful experience in our personal lives as well as in business—the tangible relating aspect.

Angie Henry, broker of New Palace Realty, is a dynamic, professional woman with a team of over twenty professionals. She has grown her business from the ground up. She does an amazing job establishing and maintaining professional relationships, and her clients love her.

When the camera comes on, and she tends to be more subdued in her message delivery. She is bilingual, charismatic, and has so much enthusiasm to offer. But it can be difficult for her clients and community to feel just how relatable she is when she freezes on camera. She used a lot of these exercises and tools, worked with me in private coaching, and has since completely transformed her on-camera confidence, grown her business, and even made two TV appearances on my shows. She has now learned to show her enthusiasm for her business and to deliver that passion in every on-camera moment. Her audience, clients, and team members now see the real Angie, and she can reach a broader market. She is a shining example of coaching success and is currently teaching these concepts to her team.

Have you ever sat through a powerful motivational speech? How did you feel afterward? What did you retain? What was the message they sent? The message was in the words they spoke, yes, but it was also in their body language, their delivery, their passion, their experience, and so on. Finding those things in yourself can help bring out a powerful message. Power is contagious; your audience should feel empowered after watching you come alive in front of them.

Think about the best restaurant you have been to. If you were to describe it to someone, would they want to go there for their next dinner out? How was your enthusiasm or message about that meal or place? Would you answer questions about it in just one sentence? Or would you be excited to share the details of the ambiance, the flavors, the drinks, the staff—whatever made it so great?

A great exercise is to do just that. Think about your favorite restaurant and the specific reasons it was so great. Create bullet points about it. Now share that out loud as if there was someone right there in front of you. Or, if you're comfortable, call a loved one or friend and tell them. Now record yourself talking about it in two minutes or less. Play it back. Would you go there after hearing it? Was your message out loud to someone the same as it was on your recording? If it was, then YES! I give you an A-plus! If it was not, then this is where we take a look at what changed. What was different for you while recording it versus saying it to a live person? This is where the techniques and self-awareness start to come together. It is an excellent "ah-ha" moment when you feel yourself letting go of the camera freeze or anxiety, and you are focused simply on the excitement for what you are sharing. It is amazing what happens when you see your messages in person and on camera shift to being received and understood.

The best way to practice is by rehearsing with close friends and family about a wide array of topics that you feel excited and eager to share about. Choose different times and settings to bring up a topic or story; see if those close to you respond differently than before. Think about your bullet points in your head. Write them down first if you need to while you are getting used to this technique.

I have the joy of working with a dynamic message giver, storyteller, and all-around great guy. Seth O'Byrne is the marketing expert for *The American Dream TV*, a top-selling luxury listing real estate agent in San Diego, California, and the host of *Hot Properties: San Diego* on HGTV. I asked him to give some insight from his experiences about delivering a message:

>
> Stories are the oldest method of conveying a message between people. It's organic, authentic, and uniquely human. For that reason, we find that telling the consumer who you are through statements falls flat compared to showing them who you are through great stories. Because stories are meant to be remembered, stories are meant to be shared. A company that masters their own great story is a company that has a real shot at being truly great.
>
> **—Seth O'Byrne**, Real Estate Agent and TV Host

Seth's insight and mastering of the message on digital media has made him millions! I have watched him grow his incredible empire and visibility for the past eight years, and I am thankful to call him a friend and grateful he wanted to share his insight with you!

Chapter 6

YOUR MESSAGE

Let me put the words in your mouth.

You are ready to master your messaging! There are media platforms we speak on now that didn't exist a few years ago. As we discussed at the beginning of this book, this technology boom has created platforms for our message from every angle imaginable. Gone are the days when showing up to a face-to-face client meeting is the only medium we can use to market ourselves and get our message delivered.

Here is what "going to a meeting" looks like for a lot of us in today's busy life:

Send an email confirming the appointment; send a text message when we're on our way; send another text that we're in the waiting room (or Zoom waiting room); then there's the interaction, the photos of the communication to post on social media, the right hashtags and shout-outs for those in the meeting, the ad boost when appropriate, and then the follow-up texts, emails, and hopefully calls . . . and that was just the start to the day! We do this process many times a day. At networking events, we are not just swapping business cards, we are asking for Instagram handles and Facebook "friending" people right on the spot. We are tagging the pictures from that event before we even leave the parking lot.

We need to be aware of how we presented our message in the midst of all that. What type of first impression did we make? What was our body language or our resting face communicating?

Exhausting, right? But this is how we live and work in our new digital world, which is why I am so passionate about helping you master your message so that you can present your best self each time you step outside (digitally or in person).

Hopefully, by this point in the book, you have been practicing your calls in the mirror, and you have rehearsed telling enthusiastic stories with your close connections for feedback on your delivery. What have you noticed at this point? This is a great time to write down what you have observed about yourself. How was it watching yourself on each call? (I am hopeful that you are doing it because it works!)

My first bit of advice for truly refining your message is this: Do not let your mouth run the show! Keep the bullet points of your message top of mind, and refer to them when interacting with others. Trust me; they will lead you to your message. We tend to want to say too much and give too much backstory. Some messages do not need a backstory, or if they do, it may only be one or two sentences. The first minute of any message is a powerful one! It is similar to the first impression we discussed in Chapter 4.

If someone asks you, "How was the event last night?"

An example that shows too much backstory may sound like this:

"Well, I was running late because my dog got out, and we had to find him. Then I couldn't find my keys, and when I got there, the valet was full, and so I had to park two blocks away. So when I got into the event, the seats were taken, and I was flustered. However, the speaker was excellent, and I enjoyed meeting some great new people who were also sitting in the back. I guess it worked out, and I enjoyed the event!"

This might seem comically long-winded, but do not laugh! I see (and hear) this all the time.

Here is a sample of the same story that is more concise, without all the unnecessary backstory:

"After some unexpected delays in getting there, I was flustered and discouraged. But my lateness put me in the back-row seats, right next to some amazing new connections. Together, we enjoyed the speaker and his message, and now I have new colleagues to network with!"

Next, I am going to get you ready for the different types of messages to be prepared for. There is the one-minute pitch, the five-minute segment, and the twenty-minute story.

The One-Minute Pitch

This is not a commercial! This refers to what you say to someone you just met in one minute or less about who you are. *Who are you?* Why should they want to keep talking to you? Can you show your passion, personality, and credibility without being scripted?

This is a tough one and takes some practice. But you will use this skill for the rest of your life—not just on camera but with everything. I have always called it the "thirty-second credibility." One of the few downsides to the prevalence of video is that our collective attention spans have grown accustomed to information being delivered to us quickly and efficiently. Consequently, our fast-paced culture has a very meager attention span. Saying what you need to say in a very short amount of time is crucial to your success.

So, in less than one minute, who are you? If someone walks up and asks what you do or who you are, you need to be able to tell them just enough information to succinctly establish credibility and start developing rapport.

Have you ever been to a webinar or in-person meeting where they ask everyone to introduce themselves and what they do? There are always those individuals that take five minutes to answer, and by the time they are done, everyone has tuned out. Or there is the participant who says their name and a one- or two-word description. Neither of these is bringing people to them like magnets. You have to find that sweet spot. That one line that makes you stand out. Everyone has one in them; you simply need to find yours!

Tell them what is it you do and what kind of hobbies you have. Maybe you have an unusual name that can be a fun and catchy introduction.

If you are a mortgage professional, instead of saying, "Hi, I'm Bob, a loan officer with XYZ bank, and I am in a cover band with my college friends. My wife hates the garage practice, but I agreed to prioritize family days and make it all work . . ." (Okay Bob, so is everyone else in this room!), let's try something else.

"Hi, I'm Bob. I help people become homeowners while pursuing my passion for music and enjoying my family of six."

The quicker you can share an interesting fact about yourself and a bit about your passions, the more likely others are to ask questions to know more. Think of people you have met and whose introductions impressed you the most. What was it they said? There is nothing wrong with using other people's ideas and changing them to fit you. Memorize your one-minute introduction. It will stay top of mind, and you will feel more confident in new environments.

The Five-Minute Segment

This segment has more complexity. When you get to have a five-minute interview, presentation, or introduction to a meeting of any kind, it is essential to use those five minutes as wisely as possible.

I had a prior *American Dream TV* guest whom I was interviewing for a TV segment, and every time I asked a question, they would spend one out of their five minutes saying, "Hi, I'm Bob. Thanks for having me . . . that's a great question, the reason I want to share today is . . ."

Okay Bob, you were already introduced, the question does not need to be repeated, and it's time to go right to the meat of your answer!

If you are talking about today's market in your area of business, expertise, industry, or region, you want to respond as specifically as possible to the question you've been asked. You need to be the expert in whatever you're speaking about. Find those things that set you apart! Maybe you are a financial planner. Then you can try starting with your credibility right off the bat.

An example for Bob, the financial planner:

"After twenty years in the financial planning industry, I have seen many ups and downs in the economy. My specialty is to communicate with my clients during those ups and downs so they are certain that I have their best interests in mind. I stay educated in the market and believe that continued, up-to-date training and knowledge can help prevent making panic decisions and keep people on their financial goals to success."

Bob does not need to talk about the three brokerages he came from before, how long it took him to build his team, or the size of his office. He needs to show his credibility and experience and how he helps people. After all, that is what they want to know. Bob, in the past, would spend two minutes describing the industry itself and all that he does for everyone in every category. Bob has now mastered his message and has increased his business and visibility because of it.

Next time, Bob can share how he advises retirees. The next message can be how he advises young adults to save for homeownership, and so on.

Each one is a small snippet of the larger picture. Whether this is Bob's video marketing on his social media or interviews on platforms or a quick segment for a podcast, each topic needs to be concise and show credibility in his field and how he makes a difference for others.

Real estate agents, we know you sell homes! We know how to get your phone number and that you want our business. How about telling us how long you have been a homeownership expert and why you love helping great people move into fantastic communities?

Tales of a lawyer—the right message wins cases:

I was doing an *American Dream TV* segment that featured a local attorney. He, like many others, was nervous in front of the camera. I spent a few minutes before going live, helping him to be comfortable and to trust my lead as the interviewer. I found out what he wanted his message to be and helped him articulate it into a four-minute segment. After we were done, he was candid with me about the nerves prior to filming and feeling tongue-tied about what he wanted to say. Once he walked into the studio with the lights and the rushed pace, he left his comfort zone. He reached out to me after with a desire to work with me (including his team).

He said, "Attorneys telling the right story and being confident in their messages win legal cases." He is right. The power of being confident in speaking and delivering the right message can mean success in any industry. Attorneys spend grueling hours getting their law degrees and learning how to be the best in their field. But the art of messaging and speaking with confidence can take them to the top of their field. I was thankful for the honesty and vulnerability of this attorney to allow me to help him.

The Longer Interview or Podcast—Twenty to Thirty Minutes

If you have the opportunity to do a feature interview, usually twenty to thirty minutes for TV or a podcast, being concise and prepared is still essential. It may sound like a long time, but twenty minutes goes fast. It allows for discussion on multiple messages and topics, differentiating it from the five-minute interviews.

This longer time is not to be wasted. It is easy to lose an audience quickly with a longer interview. This length and format requires some strategic planning, preparation, and practice to keep the messages clear and, most importantly, the energy consistent. Energy means that you are keeping the conversation exciting and flowing. Putting in some quick storytelling that pairs with your message and business can help keep the energy lifted during the interview. Hopefully, your interviewer is lively and personable, which helps keep the mood high.

Having an outline or question list will help you prepare. Practice responding to these questions to see how they fall into the allotted timeline. Find which responses need to be more concise and which can afford to be elongated. Picture how your message flows and how you would receive it as a viewer or listener. It is worth the time to do a few run-throughs to make sure your answers sound cohesive and that you are prepared to answer questions you may not have anticipated. The more you have prepared a message, included some relevant stories and facts, and thoughtfully curated your body language, the better chance you have to reach your audience and engage them for the entire interview.

In the world of podcasting, we should all be ready at a moment's notice with a fifteen- to twenty-minute story. Listen to podcasts and start to evaluate which ones you are drawn to. What about them made you listen all the way through? What did you like and not like? It will help you self-evaluate and define how you want to present yourself.

Your extra credit homework is to focus on expanding your vocabulary.

My client, Andrew Vose, is an Army veteran and real estate team leader in Colorado Springs. He brings passion, drive, and excellence to everything he does. However, he realized he was using the same words in each social media post, communication, radio show, and podcast interview. He started focusing on diversifying his vocabulary, and things slowly changed for him. I have watched him successfully transform his message and elevate his interviews with this tool.

Expanding your vocabulary can be an incredible asset for effective and powerful communication and message delivery. Think about the words you choose to use daily. Which ones seem to be on repeat and autoplay? I like to ask my coaching clients to start finding ways to replace their usual words and introduce new ones into their everyday lexicon. This will create new habits of finding creative and advanced dialogue that will set you apart from most. We all tend to get comfortable with our current vocabulary, but it is time to expand. An elevated vocabulary will make you sound polished and professional and will also keep your audience engaged. Then, when that new skill is added to your media interviews and video posts, it will be noticed, and your credibility will skyrocket.

Chapter 7

VISUALIZATION

Leave it at the door.

This is the part where I talk about overcoming that pre-speaking/pre-camera anxiety. This is the most common fear and, for many, the hardest aspect of their jobs. This is where we combine all the skills learned up to this point and synthesize them. An analogy I like to use is that of a sports team that has been practicing individual plays all week long, leading up to the big day. Finally, it's time to put all the plays into action in a culminating event: the game.

This is your game time. And in this virtual world, you will compete frequently! So how do you take these tools and deliver a new you on camera? Okay, do not put the book down when I say this, but the key is *visualization*.

Stay with me; I am going to show you some great tips and ways to keep your mind on the game and not on the practice. How do you focus on your performance and not the fans in the stands? I call this part "leave it at the door."

Visualization is the formation of a mental image of something. Psychiatrist Jennifer Baumgartner describes it as "a cognitive tool assessing imagination to realize all aspects of an object, action or outcome." Dr. Katherine Maciolek, a psychotherapist in Washington D.C., states that there is value in "using imagery before personal or professional interaction when one can imagine successfully giving a presentation or taking an exam. When involved in sports, one can mentally practice before a game, imagining catching a football or making a goal. When preparing for a difficult medical procedure, one can visualize the result of a successful outcome." For our purposes, visualization is the process of quieting the mind to mentally focus on the priorities at hand, the message you need to communicate, and your goals for how the upcoming camera appearance will go. It is essentially learning how to manifest your ideal performance.

As a professional, you are likely accustomed to juggling several tasks at once, while managing a family and maintaining an active personal life. There are understandably many things on our minds at any given time, especially given how many groups and social circles we take part in on a regular basis (community outreach, networking groups, recreation and hobbies . . . the list is endless).

Top Five Things That Distract Us From Focusing On-Camera

1. The *phone* (Every call and text will come in right before you film!)
2. Clients and co-workers
3. Family
4. Fatigue
5. Traffic—road rage

Okay, back on track. So, say you are ready to do live filming at a location to promote your business, and right before you are scheduled to film, you get three calls from clients all wanting something immediately. Also, your son called to say he got in a fender bender, and your wife texted to remind you about dinner with her parents that night.

If you are functioning in a virtual space and working from home right now, imagine that your daughter decided to dog-sit the neighbors' dogs and a construction worker is operating a jackhammer on the street outside your window. Meanwhile, you are five minutes from being on camera for an important Zoom meeting.

In both scenarios, you have practiced all the skills discussed in the previous chapters, as well as rehearsed your message; however, you rehearsed on your own time and in a controlled environment. Nine times out of ten, your real-life scenario won't be as predictable or controlled!

We have become used to being accessible 24/7. In addition to being texted, called, and e-mailed, we can be reached by a message on Facebook messenger, Instagram, WhatsApp, Twitter, LinkedIn, and several others. People tend to get impatient if we are not beholden to our phones and quick to respond, especially in any type of sales or client-oriented business. Our families also think that we can be accessible at any moment, and so we may find ourselves with a constant influx of distraction. For these reasons, it may take some time to get the hang of overcoming your on-camera nerves using the tool of visualization.

When you first begin practicing visualization, I would suggest that you "clear the noise," rendering yourself inaccessible by phone, no less than fifteen minutes before any camera appearance. Let people know you will be in a meeting and will not be accessible until you're finished. Do not check your emails, read your texts, or assess how many likes your most recent post received. There will always be some communication that you will want to handle immediately, but to properly allow yourself the time and space to practice visualizing your performance, you need to tune out temporarily. Choose the timeslot in advance (it does not necessarily need to be the fifteen minutes before your on-camera time), and give yourself those fifteen minutes as a gift to prepare.

To this day, I slip away somewhere private for ten minutes before I sing or speak publicly to clear the noise, get my head in the game, and be ready to perform. I think about who I am doing the performance for (part of my *why*), the blessing of having the opportunity, and allow myself to be the "performer" in that moment. I do the same thing before I host TV or participate in podcast interviews. It is my consistent, tested routine, and it works.

Here is a time when visualization was put to the test for me:

I was getting ready to sing the national anthem for a Navy ship's commissioning in San Diego, California. It was televised, and every top brass and city official was on deck, literally standing next to me. I had been very ill with bronchitis, and my vocal cords were fragile. I did not know if my voice was going to do what it needed to, and my insecurities started to overtake my mind. I have performed the anthem at hundreds of events over the years, including at professional sports stadiums. My visualization technique always prepared me and allowed me to do the best I could and be proud of the performance. This day was different. It was crowded, and there was nowhere for me to go to get ten minutes alone to visualize beforehand.

So I closed my eyes and went there amid the hustle and bustle of the ceremony before me. I visualized every other time that I had the honor of singing the national anthem. I pictured myself perfectly healthy and could feel myself standing in a past performance.

When I got to the podium, I looked out at the crowd, and one woman stood out. It was my friend, with whom I had done many veteran events before. She is a dynamo difference-maker in the veteran nonprofit circle; she gave me an air-kiss and hug from the crowd. That was all I needed. I found an anchor for me to focus on and remind me that I was trained for this. Voice or no voice, I was taught to work with my instrument and to deliver my best. I did it.

I have seen this same thing happen to so many just before the camera goes on. Something is wrong that day, or something distracts them, and their message and/or personality goes right out the window.

Practice is absolutely paramount with this technique. In addition to imagining the ideal performance, one method of visualization is also placing yourself in an emotional state of the past to channel the same energy in the present. To do this, you might recall some of the most joyous, energized moments of your life and mentally place yourself there! Where were you? How did you feel that day? Try to remember as many details as possible to bring yourself back to that place. Tune out all of the other noise and burdens weighing on you at that moment. They will all be there when you are done; you can tend to them later. Use these fifteen minutes before you go on camera, radio, Zoom, or whatever you are doing, to put your body in a strong, confident position. Standing or sitting, picture yourself strong. Look at your face in the mirror. Yes, flip the visor down in your car again or snatch your phone and look at your face. Look at your face while you visualize your best self.

We all have memories of strength when we accomplished something that surprised even us. That is the mindset you want to be in. Those are the memories to bring forth.

Unfortunately, visualization can be dangerous if your thoughts are not controlled. I promise if you think about being nervous or not being articulate or forgetting your message, then you likely will. To quote Henry Ford, "Whether you think you can or you think you can't, you're right."

Once you have done the work to know your face and body language, you will be able to deliver a controlled and positive message without having to consciously focus on your body language. When you have done the work to practice your first impressions, your message will flow seamlessly and readily in new situations. When you exercise your one-, five-, and twenty-minute messages, you are prepared and ready to deliver them.

Experience really can create new realities. Think of any sport or activity you tried for the first time. I remember when I tried yoga. I could not keep my balance for even one moment. I had been called a klutz my whole life, and I believed it. I could fall over my own feet at any time. I decided to tune out my past insecure and awkward self to try yoga with a new set of eyes. I started to visualize myself in class—breathing, focused, and succeeding.

Most importantly, I imagined enjoying it! The outcome was that my balance developed, evolving to the point where I didn't feel like I had to be in the back of the class anymore. I started coming to class with new confidence and began to believe in my head that I belonged and succeeded in yoga. Experiencing the growth and success created my new reality as a yogi.

At this point, I am hopeful that I have helped you get your head in the game, like a locker-room speech from a coach gets athletes focused and ready for a win. Now you deliver! You can do this! It is incredible how all these tools used together create success.

Chapter 8

ATTITUDE

*How to get the negativity out of your
media preparation.*

When we use the word *attitude*, it can sound negative. But *attitude* is a powerful word! We use it in all sorts of dimensions. Attitude simply means "state of mind."

What attitude do you have right now? Think about what state of mind you are in today. Is it peaceful, stressed, anxious, or joyous? Those are all attitudes.

To be able to identify your attitude, acknowledge how it impacts your experiences and relationships, and then intentionally controlling it is the next step in being able to positively deliver your message on camera.

My friend, Sally, has a grown son who, every time he calls, has an attitude of panic and urgency. There is always a "crisis;" this attitude shows through his voice and the pace and tone of his delivery, and he consequently comes across upset or fearful.

Sally knew that she needed to help him figure out new strategies for a happy and successful life in work and personal relationships. She started acknowledging the negative or fearful experiences he was having and reframing them to shed light on the positive elements of the situation. She would say, "Wow, it's great that you're finding out early in the relationship that this girl is not emotionally ready to commit. Isn't that wonderful that it's helping you get closer to finding the right one? Look at all you learned about yourself throughout this time with her. It is exciting to add more tools to your toolbelt that will help your future relationships."

Regarding his fear of job opportunities, she would say, "Maybe it's okay the manager of this job hasn't called you back yet. That may mean it was not the right one for you, and the right one is about to reveal itself! Think about how happy you will be when the right one comes along. You may have been spared from a job you wouldn't have found as fulfilling."

Her son responded well to this type of feedback and attitude shift. She noticed that his entire demeanor and viewpoint of the circumstance changed. She noticed he became more positive and less fearful when something around him was going wrong. Now, his mind is thinking about how excited he is to be finding that "right one," whether it is a new relationship or a new job. The disappointments are now blessings and not negatives. This type of communication worked well for Sally's son. His attitude changed. Nothing in his circumstance changed, but by seeing it through a different lens, he transformed his attitude.

I tell this story to encourage you to reflect upon the ways you can identify and transform your attitude so you may bring your best to the camera every time. Nicholas Boothman, best-selling author of *How to Make People Like You in 90 Seconds or Less*, is a brilliant communications expert, and he teaches a significant game-changing lesson in how we label attitude! He shared a great example with me. Regarding people who say they are shy, he says, "Well, that is not the case. Their attitude is cautious or reserved." If you can identify how you see yourself, how you see a situation, or how to overcome a fear—such as the fear of being on camera—then it can allow you to change your mindset. If you are reserved, which of the exercises can we use to find out what you are reserved about? Was it how you looked? Then let's find your power outfit and best look! Is it your message? Then make a list of the bullet points and practice! You're now probably a lot less reserved about that issue and not even thinking about the word *shy*. We identified the source, and we just took it out of your mind!

This is a lot to visualize, but with the combined steps, this will retrain your brain. Like I shared earlier in the book, I am not here to try to change you. I just want to help you find your *best self*! When you clear the cookies on the computer, it doesn't fundamentally change the hardware of the computer; it only helps the system run more efficiently and effectively. That's what we are doing here in this section. We are adding and modifying habits so that your system can "run cleaner," and the new attitudes can start to reveal themselves.

I Get To

Visualization can come from holding a mindset of "I get to" instead of "I have to." After twenty-nine years of parenting four kids, my perspective on what I used to think was inconvenience has drastically changed.

In the early years of child-rearing, we are tired, and many days are overwhelmed by the needs of each child, the school schedules, after-school activities, managing the home, and the demands of a career simultaneously weighing in. As a young mom, I would become frustrated and impatient quickly. I live with some regret about how I handled the kids and situations throughout those early years. My three boys are now in their early to late twenties. My youngest daughter is nearing the end of high school. My boys accurately point out that I am a different mother to her than I was to them. As I experience the last years of carpooling, backpacks, and a child's dependence upon me coming to an end, I find myself wishing I had treasured it this way with the boys. My mindset shifted. Driving the boys all around would be a "have to." Now with her, I ultimately realize that "I get to." I know that soon I will not "get to" anymore since she is learning to drive.

One day, I dropped her off at school, and ten minutes later, she called to say she had left her school project on the kitchen counter, and it was due today. She was so apologetic on the phone. I quickly returned to the school to bring it to her. As she walked up to the car door, I could see the apprehension and self-punishment in her eyes. I know this child; she strives for perfection, and the thought of forgetting something, let alone asking me to drive back, allowed her to torture herself mentally more than she deserved. I knew she needed to be encouraged. The younger me would not have caught this moment to be a blessing and let her off the hook. The old me would have been inconvenienced. This new, more grateful, and calmer me looked in her eyes and said: "Don't worry, I am so happy that I get to help my daughter today. I get to bless you today and bring you your project! Now have a fantastic day. I love you."

The relief on her face said it all. I wish I had lived in this mindset years earlier. I wish I had seen all those moments of fear, frustration, procrastination, and avoided risk-taking from the eyes of "I get to" instead of the "I have to" that used to plague me.

How much does this relate to media training and being on camera? It's everything! Remember, each of us lives with insecurities, personal struggles, past pains, and all of life's daily ups and downs. When you see people on camera, it's easy to think they don't feel insecure or that their on-camera skills come naturally. I am here to tell you, they can do it because of learned skills and practice of the techniques: visualization, self-awareness, and the power to choose one's own attitude.

There are those days when I'm off camera that I cry or feel depleted or unsure about my message. But these tools allow me to work through them and get back to the other side. The practice and success of how these tools work together will create new realities over and over. The practice will become routine. Your confidence will support your new "attitude." Once we have succeeded in something a few times, isn't it natural to be more confident? Once we have achieved something, it just becomes a new part of who we are and what we do.

Remember when you learned to swim as a child, the fear of first putting your head underwater, the first time swimming in the deep end, or your first time diving into the pool? But by the time you had mastered it, you didn't even think twice before you dove right into the deep end of the pool. You didn't have to stop and visualize how to succeed at swimming to the other side. It became automatic, second nature, something you did without thinking. Sure, you knew to be careful, to look before you dove to make sure the water was deep enough! But you were confident. You were a swimmer. That is what will start to happen with your on-camera skills! You will see new habits form that you did not think were possible.

Uncomfortable

Being "uncomfortable" seems to be another barrier that people talk to me about. I hear so many times from professionals that being on camera or speaking publicly is "out of their comfort zone." So let's talk about comfort.

In 2018, my family and I were able to experience the natural beauty of South Africa and Zimbabwe, spending time in a safari camp in the Madikwe Game Reserve. It was an incredible experience with many life-long memories and takeaways. As I watched one of the animals, it drew my attention—the giraffe. I noticed the way he was standing at the watering hole and the way he had to drink. I asked our guide to explain to me why they have to drink the way they do. The answer was surprising and a great teaching moment.

According to our guide: Due to the nature of the long legs, the giraffe has to spread them apart as wide as he can to then drop his neck down into the water. Because of this, the blood pressure in a giraffe's brain is at a different level than the rest of his body. As a result, a giraffe can only keep its head down for twenty-five seconds. In doing this, though, he creates an uncomfortable circumstance. When his neck is down, there is a pocket of blood that accumulates in the back of his neck, which can cause him to pass out. So he drinks as much as he can, and then quickly snaps his head back up to relieve the discomfort and regain equilibrium.

He has to become uncomfortable almost to the point of passing out just to get the water he needs to survive. As humans, we don't like to get uncomfortable to get what we want. We could learn a thing or two from the giraffe . . . and lean into life-bringing (or at the very least, career propelling) discomfort. It might just be exactly what we need to survive.

The mandatory shelter-in-place orders of 2020 saw most of us working from home. In the beginning, survival was the only priority. Many of us had school-aged children at home all day too (or even young infants and toddlers no longer able to attend day care.) Zoom intrusions were the norm, and we all extended each other the grace and patience we deserved as we learned to navigate this strange new world. However, at the point of writing this book, we've had over eighteen months to journey through this (now familiar) territory. While it might have been appropriate to eat a bowl of oatmeal in your virtual conference last year, it is no longer acceptable. I am the first to admit that it was initially very funny and humbling to realize that everyone in the Zoom conference had replaced the lower half of their business attire with pajama bottoms and slippers. Our world had just been turned upside down by a global pandemic, and we needed some creature comforts to assure us that although we were in uncharted territory, we could at least be comfortable. It's normal to lean into what is known and comfortable, just as it is normal to shy away from what isn't.

Almost two years later, however, it's time to accept that pajamas are no longer acceptable business attire, even if no one can see them. COVID-19 changed the way we conduct business, and virtual meetings are the new norm. This means that we need to be dressed for the camera in the same way we would be in person. We need to finish our meals ahead of time and schedule quiet, uninterrupted spaces to conduct these meetings. A child or spouse accidentally barging in on a meeting was perfectly normal when we were still scrambling to get the lay of the land. At this point, we should have a designated space for meetings in our homes or offices, free of distractions and noise, with a virtual or live background that is appropriate for our audiences.

We have spent the last year being both comfortable *and* uncomfortable. So yes, *you can learn to* become comfortable on camera! Staying in a mindset that digital media is not for you just isn't the truth. It is for everyone! We all bring something different to the virtual table, and this diversity brings life into the virtual business space. I do not want to see the same polished person in every social media feed, and neither do clients or prospective employers. The diversity that exists in the real world must also be present in the virtual world. Your personality, quirks, and individuality should not be washed out by the studio lighting.

I hope this chapter has challenged you in a few ways to think differently, to change your mindset, and to think about your camera and media opportunities as an exciting experience you "get to" have. I hope that you are ready to be like our friend, the giraffe, and get uncomfortable more often. Now, on to the studio! It is time to talk about what to expect when you walk in the doors.

Chapter 9

BEFORE THE LIGHTS

What to expect when you show up in the studio.

Okay, now you're ready. You have done the exercises, and you are ready to get on camera. You are well prepared for that upcoming podcast or the next big Zoom meeting. I hope you are excited about where we are going now in this chapter: to the studio! Whether it is a significant network, podcast, independent studio, or your home Zoom, let's take a look at each of these and what to expect.

Here is a story about a studio "fail" that still gives me the giggles to this day.

Where Did Sexy Go?

On an average day in-studio, filming and hosting for *The American Dream TV*, I was wired up and ready to greet my next guests. The interviews were done with me at the home studio in San Diego, and the guests were patched in from our partner studios in different cities around the country.

My usual routine is to be in my seat, ready to go while watching on my monitor as the guests get "mic'd up" and patched through to see and hear me and do the interview. What most of the guests don't realize is that I can see and listen to them before they can ever see or hear me. This allows me to get a good feel for my incoming guests and to see if they are nervous or need any special help or attention from me to have their interview go as well as possible.

On this day, two gentlemen were getting settled into their seats in their distant studio. As I watched, I could see they were good friends—they were lighthearted, had great senses of humor, and they looked relaxed and polished for the interview. I was not worried about these two. I figured it would be a quick, personable segment.

They even complimented each other on how they looked. The one guy looked to the other and said, "You look sexy," and then that second guy said to the first man, "Hey, you're looking pretty sexy too." So, they are both feeling "sexy" and ready for the interview.

My producer, Carlos, says in my ear, "Okay, Amy, are you ready for me to patch them through to you?" I confirmed. Sexy 1 and Sexy 2 can now see and hear me. I briefly went over the topic questions with them and said,

"Okay guys, let's get started." I gave a quick introduction of the guys on camera and thanked them for being on the show that day.

Somehow, in that quick timeframe, they both developed a "deer in the headlights" look on their faces, and I could barely get them to answer the questions. They were monotone in their delivery, stiff in their posture, and their personalities were missing. The same guys who were full of personality moments before had disappeared. *Where did sexy go?* It was a very stale interview, and their message was lost. If only they had kept the "sexy" mindset, they would have been a hit that day!

This is why I am teaching you these proven techniques: to show you how not to let that happen to you and to paint you a picture of what to expect in each of these scenarios. First, let's think about the first time you went to an amusement park. I live near Disneyland, so I am going to use that park for reference. All of the commercials for the park and the testimonies from patrons who had gone have led up to an incredible anticipation for the day. You pack a backpack to prepare for anything. It includes a sweatshirt, sunscreen, bottled water, energy bars, hand sanitizer (yes, that should have been a habit before COVID-19!) and are set for the day!

If you were a young kid, then your mom had all this set for you! You were so excited, picturing a day of nothing but fun! So for you who had the amusement park adventures, what did you look like at the end of the day? Think about how tired and worn out you were. What happened in between? The rides were incredible! You did not know what it was going to feel like standing in line for an hour for each ride in the heat, nor did you expect the amount of walking you would do, and also you might not have worn the right shoes, and the food costs a fortune! You didn't get to try all the goodies you wanted? Got a stomachache from the adrenaline? Yep, most likely . . . A day at the park is excellent, but at the same time, you probably got a little beat up.

Welcome to the media! It's like a day at Disneyland with all that comes with it!

I am going to help you prepare for some of those stomach aches and tired-feet moments that lie ahead. Don't say I didn't tell you! Here it is.

Major Network TV Studio

Let's first get you prepared for the TV studio. Whether this is a morning news show or a private studio for a unique program, they all have a similar vibe and way of running that I am going to walk you through.

I will use a TV news studio for our first example. These studios have lots of team members and staff that all hold a different role to keep this fast-paced machine running smoothly. These teams are no-nonsense. They do this every day, all day, and on time, sticking to strict time schedules for local and national networks. They do not care if it took you longer to park; they do not care if you want to fix your hair or lip gloss. They have a tight schedule, and they are doing you the favor of putting you on air! They expect that you will be polished, ready, and that you have done this a million times. Yes, of course, some will have a friendly staff member available for some gentle handling with you, and they are trained at having those needed people skills, but be prepared to be focused, on time, and on task.

You will arrive and be greeted at a lobby and check in. A team member will escort you, most likely to a "green room." You will then sit and wait for the next greeting. They will most likely inform you of how long you will be sitting there and when to be ready to be escorted to the filming studio. This green room time is very crucial for your mindset and your outcome! I cannot stress enough to use this time wisely! Do *not* start checking your emails or voicemails! Yes, go ahead and take a selfie, text your loved one that you checked in and are ready, but that should be it. This is the locker room before walking onto the field for the Super Bowl! If your head is not already in the game and ready for the seat, then you will be very thrown off of your game when they sit you in the chair!

This is the time to use all the exercises we have worked on.

Yes, you look fabulous!

You planned your outfit so you know it works!

You know your message. You have been practicing it over and over, and you have watched videos and have been training to understand what you are saying.

Yes, you have an attitude of "I GET TO!"

And yes, you know that you are about to make a great first impression!

All you need to think about is breathing in and out fully, keeping your message top of mind, and controlling your body language. To the best of your ability, keep your personal life, email inbox, and any other potential distractions out of mind for the duration of your segment.

Now, allow me to guide you through the initial moments of walking into the studio. It is bigger than you pictured. There are cords everywhere, and the studio crew is rushing around like a fire drill is taking place. They do not have time for your questions. They will expect you to listen and follow directions. First, they will tell you exactly where to sit, test your microphone, and verbally lead you. Take direction, stay humble, and say thank you. If you are a great guest to work with, it is a lot more likely to be asked to return! Let them see that you came prepared. You had media coaching! You are ready to do this.

When you are at the news desk, you'll be listening to the segment that is recording live just to the right of you. Maybe it is the weather or traffic. Suddenly, they transition to a commercial break. Now, your heart is really racing. You know that after that commercial, the camera is going to be on you. The host is going to do a quick intro, go to her lead question, and boom—you are live!

The lights are *hot*! And they are *bright*! If you prepare mentally for that ahead of time, it will not throw you off. Here is an example of good preparation.

My husband, Brad, spent thirty years in federal law enforcement in Los Angeles, California, working some of the most high-profile national and international investigations throughout the country. Throughout his career, he was a SWAT team leader, worked gang/narcotic units, the bomb unit, the counterterrorism unit, and traveled the world conducting international training assignments. To say he is confident would be an understatement. He could have written a book about his years as a federal agent. As an expert in these categories, he often gets calls from local and national news media to be an expert advisor on national topics in headlining stories. He had to learn how to be media-ready at a moment's notice and has since had to master these same techniques for success.

One of those times he was called upon, he was sound asleep, and they needed an expert for the 5:00 a.m. news. Thankfully, this was a "call-in," so he was able to do it with bed head and in his shorts. However, he had to know his message with two minutes' notice and be articulate and ready for the interview. I don't know how I would have done at that early hour because I do not always know my own name at 5:00 a.m.! But he was used to middle-of-the-night emergency calls, and he handled this one perfectly.

The next call came from CNN; they wanted to send a camera crew to the house to interview him briefly. He quickly learned how to choose the best suit, find the perfect spot in the house, and master a professional interview as if he were in their multimillion-dollar studio. If you are called as an expert, you never know where they are going to film you. We have had news crews at our front door, back patio, and living room, all to get his expert advice on major national security topics. And I thought I was the TV host in the family! Since retirement, he has been getting the spotlight and had to learn how to be media-ready. I do hope that I get some small credit for being his on-site media coach, as I did help him learn about his resting face and body language, and I have fine-tuned his camera placement for Skype interviews. Another time, NBC sent a limo to take him to the local news station where he was treated like a rock star and experienced for himself the hot lights and fast-paced pressure of being in a significant network studio. His preparation, awareness of what to expect, and expertise in his field of knowledge made a world of difference.

Okay, now that I've finished patting myself on the back for transforming a federal agent into a master of media, here is an example of one of his interviews on a major national network (CBS) that could have gone poorly had he not been prepared. This was *live* national news. He was in position at a local CBS studio, being patched in along with one other person from another studio in a different city for a discussion panel on a national security topic. He was "mic'd up" and on camera when his audio failed. In mid-interview, they immediately rewired him with back-up audio while he had to continue to follow the questioning, staying focused and centered during the process. This was all in about a fifteen-second timeframe. When he was fully back up and could hear the host, the discussion was halfway in, and he had to be on-point with his message, regardless of not being able to hear part of the interview. This may not seem complicated, but picture yourself in that situation. How would your message, body language, and concentration hold up? I think many of us, regardless of training, would have been at least momentarily distracted by the setback. Had he not been prepared and known his main message better than the back of his hand, the outcome could have been disastrous. He handled it like a pro, despite disliking being behind the camera. Unlike me—I love my job! When the camera is on, I come alive, like I am right where I was born to be. Like many of the business professionals I have interviewed on my show, he does not like it, but he figured out how to do it, and the audience get to see the polished, finished product. My point is that training pays off—like it did for my husband and the many other professionals who take the time to prepare.

I have worked with many people who say they do not like being on camera, but they do it. With practice, training, and repetition, they have learned to be good at it, and it has helped their careers. I am sure that athletes do not always "like" the intense training, but they love the results. These moments of uncertainty can happen in any media format. If you rehearsed your message thoroughly, you are more likely able to get past obstacles or unforeseen glitches. The preparation breeds success! You will feel so different after this experience when you see how prepared you were, how you handled it, and, hopefully, how you grew to love it!

Podcast or Independent Studio

The pace and hustle at a podcast or independent studio will most likely be a little more comfortable than a major network studio, depending on the size. However, if this is your first studio experience, then all of the big-studio preparation above will apply to you just as much. You will still want to get there early and have time to get your head in the game. *No checking emails or your phone!*

If it is a podcast studio, many still do video recording and live streaming of the podcast. So come dressed and polished just as you would for the camera. Like we discussed in preparing for the long messaging interviews, doing a podcast or radio segment means that you need to actively keep your energy up. You are sitting up straight, smiling, and being expressive with your message. Even if the camera is not on, the delivery will be much better with a lively personality. Don't forget to sit close to the microphone.

Your Zoom Meetings or Home Camera

The preparation for your home on-camera meetings is just as necessary! Remember that even though you are at home and comfortable in your socks, this on-camera appearance still requires that you keep in mind first impressions, concise introductions, and delivering a powerful message. Even if you are a meeting contributor, make sure you are ready to articulate professionally.

Take time to set up and turn on your camera in advance to take a look at yourself and your surroundings.

Notice the lighting, positioning, and background. Check your Wi-Fi connection as well so you have full connection and speed for your calls and filming.

Camera

Your camera should be at eye level, so that you are not looking up or down to see it. A simple solution for framing can be to place your laptop or smartphone on boxes until your device is level with your face and not pointed up your nostrils or to the floor. Make sure to frame your face in the middle of the screen so that it is balanced, like you would do for a photo.

Lighting

If you are using the natural light in the room, it needs to come toward you, not from behind you. If you sit in front of a window that is bringing light behind you, it will wash you out like a ghost. You want to find any spot where light can be on your face and not behind you for balance. The best way to do this is to walk around with your device and find the best spot where you can see your face with the most contrast and natural color.

Ring lighting is the best invention to come along for filming and working in our home studios. There are multiple sizes and price options to meet any budget. A ring light set up just behind the camera makes a tremendous difference in properly lighting your face and making you look prepared and professional. It is a must-have item and worth the investment. They are very affordable and can plug right into a USB. Some even come with a full-sized tripod with a phone holder in the middle to make professional, well-lit videos right from any cell phone.

Audio

Any audio is better than no audio at all. Investing in a professional podcast microphone is great, especially if you are going to consistently be on camera while working from home. Invest in a name brand Bluetooth earpiece, if possible. If not, any less expensive brand will still achieve clear, unmuffled audio. You want to use a headset, even if it is wired to the phone, for the best audio. Trying to film a cell phone video when you are standing away from it does not work. You will lose all your audio and the message will not be delivered. You may have the best location, set up, lighting, and tripod for the shot, but if you don't have a microphone, you'll lose good audio, and your message and audience will be also be lost.

Setting up the right camera angle, light, and audio can be very inexpensive and still look and sound great. If you want to invest in higher-tech options for an authentic stay-at-home studio, you will not regret it. Our virtual world will continue, and these assets to your business will be truly worth it.

Green Screen

If you do not have a background that works for you, there are inexpensive green screen options to buy. You can now also apply a virtual background in many virtual meeting platforms. The green screen is better than the background option that comes with Zoom. It tends to look blurry, and many times people tend to disappear into it while on camera. If the virtual screen is blurry or you disappear, then it takes away from the crisp, professional look. Sometimes, they work, but you always need to test it first before you go live to make sure.

These extras will help you feel confident and show your best self every time. Today's technological world allows us the opportunity to have home studios in any space.

How You Look

Now that you have your technology set-up or you are ready for the major studios, let's talk about how to dress and prepare yourself. Different settings will require different wardrobes. Whether it's a professional suit and tie, a dress or a pantsuit for ladies, business casual, or casual attire for a field shoot, dress for the location. Here are a few suggestions to help you look your best.

First, always ask what the attire is for a media appearance if you are at all unsure. With any dress code, solid colors always look the sharpest. Try to avoid white and or stripes if you can help it. Try to have clothes that are fitted nicely to your body shape. It is easy for something flowy to give you the appearance of being "puffed up" when you did not mean for it to.

My best advice regarding what to wear is simple: Choose an outfit that makes you feel confident and like your most authentic self when you wear it. The one that you know fits right, looks right, and that you don't have to adjust or fix while wearing. Women, we are most guilty of this. We may have an outfit that we love and that looks good, but only when we are standing still. Does it fall down the shoulder or ride up when you sit? You will want to wear it in a few positions and make sure that, if sitting, it is still the look you want.

Take a few pictures in the clothes sitting and standing to see how it will look and feel for your appearance. Something may look great for a dinner out, but on camera, it may wash you out or just not look the same. Preparation and selection before your appearance is key.

Hair and Makeup

Style your hair the way you do most of the time. You do not want to have a great interview with a new hairstyle that does not truly represent what you look like regularly. If you are building your brand and your following, you want others to see a consistent version of you. That doesn't mean you can't change it around once in a while, but don't go to a new hairdresser to have them do your hair for on-camera appearance, come out looking like someone else, and never look like that again. You being *you* is usually your best self.

Makeup . . . you want to wear a little more than you wear for an average day. If you do not wear any, then at least add color to your cheeks and lips, or your face will disappear. You want your features to stand out. It may feel uncomfortable at first to have more makeup on than you are used to, but when you see the footage played back, you will see that it made you look natural. Lighting will wash you out. Even the at-home ring lights will wash you out, and you want to accent your face. For makeup, the same advice applies: don't have your face done by someone who has not done your makeup before. You want to look like yourself on camera. Just an additional amount on the eyes, lips, and cheeks will ensure that you don't look washed out on camera.

Practice, practice, practice! Do a Zoom with the family and record it. Take pictures in your clothes, hair, and makeup under lighting and see how it looks to you. You must review your work and your look! You will be much better prepared, self-aware, ready to appear, and ready for any studio.

Chapter 10

YOU ARE READY FOR THE LIGHTS, CAMERA, AND ACTION

At this point, you should be well prepared to deliver your professional message by utilizing any of the great media training options I have taught you. I get so excited to see people grow and find their new and authentic selves on camera. I know you can do it (whatever *it* is for you)! We can accept that life is always changing.

You may have picked up this book and thought you were only going use it for your online presence. Or maybe you thought you only have a face for radio. We can all be sure that the future is exciting and unknown. Who would have thought back when the flip phone was popular that someday you would be reading a book to help you make better videos to improve your business? Did you imagine when you were making your home family videos that someday being on a camera would be the primary way of communicating throughout the world? Back then, it was only for TV newscasters and actors.

We never dreamed that our lives would evolve into this virtual way of living. But here it is! It is hard enough getting my eighty-year-old parents to use Facetime or Zoom without only being able to see the ceiling. If they can try it, so can you! This is the time to embrace change. People are getting left behind if they are not advancing in these specific skills. Saying that you are not technology-savvy does not cut it anymore. Everyone hopefully has a teenager or millennial around that would be happy to set up your technology and show you how to navigate operating it. If you don't have one of them around, you can teach yourself nearly anything online. I recommend watching tutorials about your specific equipment and practice until you're comfortable enough to troubleshoot any issues that may arise.

You have walked with me through the training and lessons in this book. At this point, you have likely begun the exercises and realized how crucial they are to your success. The work you have done here is not just going to change your camera presence, but hopefully also the way *you* see yourself! You should feel different . . . confident and ready! Did you ask your loved ones to help you, as I advised in Chapter 3, by improving your ability to listen and communicate? These steps, if you continue, will be produce ongoing transformation and will ensure your success in this new digital media world.

What you learned with me is the same technique you would use for training to run a marathon: practice and preparation. You practice and train over and over again, perhaps completing your first race in six hours. By continuing to train and practice, you might then run this same distance in just over four or five hours the next time. You have improved—the practice and training have paid off. Media training is no different. This is my self-awareness, first impression, message delivering, media-ready training manual that you can refer to over and over. You are going to be celebrated in your social settings as you help others when the camera turns to *on*. *You* will be the media-ready pro! You can take these same techniques and help others around you.

As you learned in Chapter 2, in the past twenty years, there have been countless technological advancements, but one thing remains the same. People want to work with those they know, like, and trust. What I hope I have done for you is taught you how to be the same lovable you— but on camera. I hope I helped you prepare the message that was already inside you, but now, you are ready to deliver concisely and powerfully. You are prepared to take advantage of all the social media, TV, video, podcast, and radio outlets that are there for you if you choose! Do not let an opportunity go by just because you were too uncertain about being on camera. Do not waste your next Zoom meeting with the wrong camera angle or lighting or leave a bad first impression. You are ready! Do not miss an opportunity in your community to be a difference-maker and help others share their compelling stories. You are ready.

All of these possibilities are open and endless. Preparation, like with anything else, is the key. Once you train to be a marathon runner, you are ready. You can sign up for any marathon you want.

It is important you continue to practice these exercises! A compelling way to keep this "new you" going is to find ways within your business and social groups to make videos! Share your messages and stories. Find out what others are doing on social media and other media platforms. Stay connected on the camera!

My best friend is Cheryl Leon. She is a talented photographer and makes magic with her camera. But there is something about her that is so special. She uses her gift of photography and brings out the brightest and best in others! She is always finding the best angles and features of those photographs. I have had the privilege of standing alongside her when she is working significant events, headshot parties with people sitting down every fifteen minutes to work with her. But this is no JC Penny "move along" shuffle set up. Everyone who sits with her is treated as if they are a runway model in Milan. I have watched her take someone nervous about how they look, smile, and sit, and turn them into masterpiece headshots. I have seen these photos used by many of our colleagues in numerous industries, and they are still using them as their primary marketing headshot. What is so different? She sees in them what they did not see in themselves. She brings out the light in each and every person in her lens. It is like magic to watch!

Now you have had a chance to not only see yourself in that lens but to take this training and help others. Not only will your own confidence grow, but as we've discussed, this on-air anxiety is more common than most realize. You can become the go-to expert in your circle on how to be great on camera, how to do radio and podcasts, and how to record those cell phone videos like a pro!

The one thing we can all be assured of is that change is constant. Who could have imagined thirty or forty years ago how we would be communicating today, digitally and virtually, through small electronic devices like phones and watches? Technology is advancing at an exponential rate. One can only imagine that it's not too long before we will be having meetings where everyone is sitting around a table in a boardroom as if actually there, all from the comfort of our home or office by way of advanced 3D holographic screens. Whichever medium is used to communicate, these same skills and techniques I have shown you here will prepare you to master your own virtual world in any environment.

Take this training and make it yours; use it to help others. Take these skills that took me twenty years of trial and error to master to not only improve your confidence and comfort while in front of the camera, but also to use as a way to grow your own networking and business opportunities. Business is built on relationships; relationships are built on trust. Developing a professional message is what gets people talking about you in a favorable way. This can only be achieved through dedication, passion, and hard work! Preparation and training are the hallmarks of excellence, just listen to what Will Smith attributes his worldwide success to: "I've always considered myself to be just average talent and what I have is a ridiculous insane obsessiveness for practice and preparation."

Now, you are prepared and ready for the new digital media marathon! Congratulations! I am cheering you on the entire way. This virtual world will only continue to grow and expand. Grow with it! Let us embrace it together. You are now the master of your own digital and virtual world.

Lights, Camera, Action!

Amy Scruggs

To learn more about
Professional Media Coaching go to:

www.amyscruggsmedia.com

About the Author

Amy uses her twenty years as a Media Executive, TV host, recording artist, public speaker, corporate spokesperson, and business professional, to help others present and communicate a concise and professional message, whether you are on-camera with network TV, interviewed by a major news or entertainment outlet, filming a corporate video, ZOOM call, podcast, social media marketing or in person public speaking appearance. As a Media Professional, Amy is known as the "Voice and Face" of Mutual of Omaha Mortgage, where she writes, directs, and hosts a national digital marketing campaign for a Fortune 500 company; she is also the in-house Media Coach for senior company executives and top sales performers. She is the current host for the national TV show, "Financing the American Dream", which airs on CNBC & Travel channel. Her hosting credits includes the parent TV show The American Dream, Lifestyles San Diego, and the Retiring Right Show. Amy has been providing media coaching and training to corporate and private clients by providing both individual and team training seminars & workshops, as well as for business executives and entrepreneurs, who are looking to enhance their virtual or digital media skills. She also advises entrepreneur clients and startup companies on messaging, branding and how to develop their own digital marketing strategies. Sharing the same tips and techniques she teaches her private clients she learned from years of being in front of and behind the camera. Amy is also a classically trained pianist and vocalist. She has over fifteen years of professional singing experience performing in front of large audiences. Amy previously toured the national country music circuit where she opened for many country music greats like Trace Adkins, Clint Black, Charlie Daniels, Phil Vassar, and many more. It is the culmination of these diverse backgrounds, as both a sales business executive, TV Host, and her years as a national recording artist and musician, that has allowed her to become one of the most sought-after media coaching and training professionals today.

To learn more about Media Coaching & Training for Professionals go to:

amyscruggsmedia.com

A free ebook edition is available with the purchase of this book.

To claim your free ebook edition:

1. Visit MorganJamesBOGO.com
2. Sign your name CLEARLY in the space
3. Complete the form and submit a photo of the entire copyright page
4. You or your friend can download the ebook to your preferred device

Morgan James BOGO™

A **FREE** ebook edition is available for you or a friend with the purchase of this print book.

CLEARLY SIGN YOUR NAME ABOVE

Instructions to claim your free ebook edition:
1. Visit MorganJamesBOGO.com
2. Sign your name CLEARLY in the space above
3. Complete the form and submit a photo of this entire page
4. You or your friend can download the ebook to your preferred device

Print & Digital Together Forever.

Snap a photo

Free ebook

Read anywhere